Woven through the unassuming simplicity of a fable, *Into the WILD* speaks to the heart of workplace culture. Sharing a powerful narrative to illustrate the importance of leadership, inclusion, shared accountability, and psychological safety at work, this book resonates with the collective experiences of many professionals as they navigate the modern-day workplace.

Incorporating the WILD Framework to start practically applying lessons learnt, this book provides the foundations to start the conversation on creating and sustaining a positive and impactful coaching culture.

— **Jennifer Taylor**
Executive and Leadership Coach
ICF Member, GENOS certified

A simple and fun book to read and understand, yet highly practical, leveraging the WILD Framework to drive a coaching culture in tomorrow's enterprises. *Into the WILD* highlights why adopting a coaching culture in organisations is so important today. The book brings this to life in a fun way with the animal characters. The authors emphasise the need for consistent conversations and interactions in order to appreciate the dynamic situation at the grassroots level. They also stress the ability to quickly create a simple and new vocabulary to align the team which then drives culture transformation. *Into the WILD* reminds everyone to keep the end in mind when creating a coaching culture, while appreciating the art of collective leadership and wisdom. As a leader, I firmly believe that a coaching culture creates an environment of interaction and trust where engagement across all functions happens seamlessly and organically. A trusting environment is the foundation to driving clarity in purpose and transparency in the organisation.

— **Alvin Ng**
Former General Manager, GE Digital, Asia
Associate Adjunct Professor, Nanyang Business School

I recommend *Into the WILD* partly because of the passion of the people who wrote the book. It is not written in a traditional academic format. It is, instead, written by people who have seen and lived the challenges of working within large corporates. Many books are written by academics who have ideas on leadership, organisational culture, and change but have not been impacted by these challenging dynamics on a daily basis and gone on to survive them. The authors have more than survived. They have used their experience to help others recognise, in a fun way, how they can own their power and bring about the needed changes. The story and images draw us into the material in a different way from many coaching texts and brings to life the challenges of the last year through the Covid crisis. The characters in the book, their insights and growth, could be written about further as we move into a post-Covid crisis world.

The following key messages in the book are universal needs for leaders: capacity to self-reflect, expansion of self-awareness, awareness of the impact of self on others, awareness of the power of the system in any organisation, conscious relations with self and others, and an ability to own limitations and ask for help as a leader.

— **Anne Welsh**
MA Creative Supervision, University of Chichester, England, UK
UKCP Accredited Psychotherapist, APECS
Accredited Executive Coach and Supervisor

I really enjoyed the book, *Into the WILD*, which is presented in the format of a short crisp interesting fable. Fantastic learnings are delivered in an easy-to-understand and implementable approach. If you desire to be a part of a company or a team where there is an equal engagement among the leaders, the employees, and the customers then this book is a brilliant start!

Into the WILD unfolds how embracing a coaching culture helps employees of the WILD Company in their transformational journey from a toxic culture to one that embraces curiosity, courage, and collaboration. This gives an opportunity to every employee to learn and contribute while playing an equal role in the success of the organisation. Kudos to the authors for such a splendid work!

— Dr Deepa Desai
Founder & CEO, D Cube Consultancy; 2019 HBA Luminary;
2020 PharmaVOICE 100 Most Inspiring Leaders; Physician

Into the WILD is a guide to the benefits of a coaching culture, for individuals and their organisations. But it's no ordinary guide. It starts with a fable, which cleverly uses real-life examples to show how cross-functional collaboration, asking the right questions, and listening to everyone—regardless of their seniority or background—enables successful outcomes. The book introduces a simple, four-step WILD Framework that can help leaders create a coaching culture by asking insightful questions, modelling the right behaviours, and using the right language to involve and engage their teams. A compelling read that inspires action.

— Birte Sebastian
Global Communications Director, Multinational Company

In today's turbulent world, ever bigger demands are put on leadership, be it individuals or teams. *Into the WILD* provides an exceptionally entertaining and accessible story for executives to familiarise themselves with the WILD approach to executive coaching. By telling this story in fable form, the writers have woven the concept of diversity into the book, in a way that readers can easily identify with, without prejudice or judgement.

Into the WILD is a powerful book that invites people at all levels of organisations to embrace coaching for themselves and their teams. Better people make better business for a better world, and *Into the WILD* will certainly make a contribution to that.

> — **Piet Coelewij**
> **Non-executive Director and Investor, former Philips, Amazon and Sonos senior executive**

Into the WILD is an easily accessible and enjoyable story that sets up the WILD Framework to help organisations create a problem-solving culture. Culture and the ability to successfully navigate challenges are so critical as we go through the Fourth Industrial Revolution. There has never been a time in which organisations have faced so much change and monumental challenges. The WILD Framework, told through the *Into the WILD* story, provides a straightforward way for organisations and teams to deal with our tumultuous times.

> — **Phil Ventimiglia**
> **Chief Innovation Officer, Georgia State University**

Into the WILD

Creating a Coaching Culture at the Workplace

**CHEONG CHOY KIEW,
AILEEN CHEE & ADRIAN LIM**

Candid Creation Publishing

First published 2021

Candid Creation Publishing books are available through most major bookstores in Singapore. For bulk order of our books at special quantity discounts, please email us at enquiry@ candidcreation.com.

INTO THE WILD

Author   : Cheong Choy Kiew, Aileen Chee & Adrian Lim
Publisher   : Phoon Kok Hwa
Editor   : Patricia Ng
Cover designer : Jeraldine Boh
Layout   : Corrine Teng
Illustrations   : Jeraldine Boh
Published by   : Candid Creation Publishing LLP
                    167 Jalan Bukit Merah
                    #05-12 Connection One Tower 4
                    Singapore 150167
Website   : www.candidcreation.com
Facebook   : www.facebook.com/CandidCreationPublishing
Email   : enquiry@candidcreation.com

National Library Board, Singapore Cataloguing in Publication Data

Names: Cheong, Choy Kiew. | Chee, Aileen, author. | Lim, Adrian, 1968- author.
Title: Into the WILD : creating a coaching culture at the workplace / Cheong Choy Kiew, Aileen Chee & Adrian Lim.
Description: Candid Creation Publishing LLP, 2021. | Includes bibliographic references.
Identifiers: OCN 1259033513 | ISBN 978-981-18-0912-5 (paperback)
Subjects: LCSH: Employees--Coaching of.
Classification: DDC 658.3124--dc23

CONTENTS

FOREWORD

You are in for a real treat.

Welcome to an entertaining, educational, easy, and engaging read. The message, the medium, and the practical suggestions of *Into the WILD* offer something for everyone. No matter what your learning preferences, age, or experiences are, you will take away unforgettable images, insights, theories, a desire to "try out", and practical tools that you can apply tomorrow in your team, your organisation, community associations, and even your family to create coaching conversations.

This book will grab you.

As someone who has been in the coaching business for more than forty-five years, I was quickly captured by the creativity and simplicity of the storytelling abilities of these three authors.

So who are the authors? I have had the privilege of working closely with Choy Kiew, one of the three authors, for more than ten years and have seen her passion and ability to create coaching conversations and cultures wherever she's worked. More recently, I have come to see the same passion and similar histories from Aileen and Adrian, Choy Kiew's co-authors. Together they have combined their talents to bring this beautiful book to life.

"The Wild Company" is a fable that gives all of us an understanding of what can happen when a "coaching culture" is nurtured to transform the life of any organisation. The animal characters resemble real life characters that all of us have seen. Readers will be gripped by the crises, twists and turns of events as the characters develop a new way to communicate and build a coaching culture. We can see ourselves—the way we are and the way we can become through the characters of this fable.

Change is inevitable and coaching conversations can produce those special ingredients that make organisational life exciting and sustainable. So, what is a "coaching conversation"? How will we know it when we see it? Both from the book and in a coaching conversation with the authors, I discovered that a coaching conversation is where curiosity, care, appreciation, understanding, empathy, reflective listening, respectful challenge, and the suspension of judgement can all co-exist. In essence, coaching conversations are learning conversations. Organisations that actively promote coaching conversations will naturally see increased engagement, improved morale, higher productivity, a reduction in employee turnover, greater profits, and much more fun. Who doesn't want that?

Moreover, the authors do much more than tell a good story. They also introduce a sound formula that we, the readers, can use to build a coaching culture wherever we are. The four parts of this simple yet powerful formula are Awareness, Investigation, Language, and Deployment. Like with any change process, the first step is Awareness. There is nothing better to stimulate change than a good conversation. Unfortunately, most good conversations—coaching conversations, that is—happen most frequently in informal settings like during coffee breaks or over lunch or going on walks with friends. It is these settings that open the door for coaching conversations to naturally appear. One of our challenges is to make these accidental coaching conversations more intentional. It can be done. Once this happens, the other three steps come to life.

Why is this book a must-read? It is not a piece of academic literature. The first part of the book offers a light-hearted view of the corporate jungle where animals take on different roles as in multinational organisations, non-governmental organisations, and families. The second part introduces a framework—aptly named WILD—that professionals, senior executives, leaders, managers, and other professionals from Organisational Development, Human Resource, as well as Learning and Development can use to create a coaching culture in the workplace.

And the authors walk the talk. They come together every Friday morning to discuss and co-create solutions for their clients. At every client-facing opportunity, all three authors are present either in person or virtually. They leverage and build on each other's strengths and capabilities using exactly what they write about—coaching conversations.

What should you, the reader, bear in mind as you read this book? To maximise your takeaway, I suggest that you first reflect on your own professional and private lives. Then ask yourself the following questions: What are some of the challenges and opportunities that I am facing? What is holding me and my team or organisation back? What needs to change? What do I want to change? What will I change? With these questions at the back of your mind—as they were on mine—you will have a rich experience, indeed.

The bottom line is that through the power of coaching conversations, corporations, governmental bodies, non-governmental entities, religious organisations, and families can become more engaging, profitable, and fun environments for everyone—irrespective of level, function, or role.

Enjoy your read!

Ernie Turner
President, Leadership In Motion (LIM); Author
and co-author of several books; Avid Learner;
Gardener; Scuba Diver; and Keynote Speaker

INTRODUCTION

Having worked together as members of an eight-person organising committee to deliver an overwhelmingly successful International Coaching Federation (ICF) Week in 2020 (ICW 2020), we—Adrian, Aileen, and Choy Kiew—decided to continue our weekly Friday morning over-Zoom conversations to minimise painful withdrawal symptoms we were experiencing upon completion of the event.

The three of us had developed great chemistry when working together on ICW 2020 and so it was a natural progression to continue to get to know each other and consider potential opportunities to journey together to grow our coaching competencies.

What transpired was a common passion and aspiration to make the world a better place for all Singaporeans, and the world. We wanted to share our knowledge and experience in coaching and the importance of creating a coaching culture in a simple and relatable way with our readers.

What is a coaching culture? In his book *Creating A Coaching Culture* (2012), Peter Hawkins defines it as such: "A coaching culture exists in an organisation when a coaching approach is a key aspect of how the leaders, managers, and staff engage and develop all their people and engage their stakeholders in ways that create increased individual, team, and organisational performance and shared value for all stakeholders."

Fundamentally, this means that coaching conversations are happening at every level in the organisation, with peers, teams, line managers, within functions and cross-functionally. It is not just the privileged few, the talents, or the high performers that experience coaching. Everyone in the organisation has the potential to experience coaching and partake in coaching conversations. The possibilities are limitless.

Why is creating a coaching culture in any organisation important? The ICF, together with the Human Capital Institute (HCI), conduct annual research surveys on creating coaching cultures in organisations. In its 2019 report entitled *Building Strong Coaching Cultures for the Future*, organisations with strong coaching cultures achieved higher outcomes in all dimensions—including profitability, productivity, customer satisfaction, talent attraction, shareholder value—compared to other organisations.

We would like to invite you, the Reader, to first read this book in its entirety, starting with the Fable followed by the Framework that we have created. The Framework and concepts that we share can be used to start creating a culture of coaching within your own organisation. This Framework is applicable at the individual, team, and organisational level.

We have created fictitious characters in the form of animals living in the wild. In this fast-paced society where changes can and have taken place in the twinkling of an eye, we may sometimes feel like we are living in a jungle where animal-like instincts dominate our thoughts and actions. And so the idea of a fable came to mind.

The characters in this Fable do not in any way represent any individuals known to the authors. Some of the episodes in the Fable are, however, based on the authors' real-life experiences and are told in a way to bring out the issues and lessons to be learnt. We believe that these issues are common in the workplace and we share how these turned out through the various interventions.

This book was conceived during the Covid-19 Circuit Breaker in Singapore. The three of us initially met via Zoom. Up to that point, Adrian had never ever met Aileen or Choy Kiew in person. The moment Phase II of the Circuit Breaker began, we met in person at Aileen's home. The rest is history.

As you start to work towards creating a coaching culture within your team or organisation, we welcome you to send us an email at **contact@thecoachingculture.co** to share your reflections and insights gained, anytime.

The
WILD Company

01
PROLOGUE

CRISIS!

The Messenger was flying wildly through the corridors. "Oh dear! Oh dear! We're in trouble! We're in deep trouble!"

"Where is Govind? Where is our CEO? Where is he? Where, where, where is he? Oh dear, oh dear, oh dear!!"

Govind and the SET—Senior Executive Team—were meeting to plan their strategy for the next business cycle. Business was good, they were diversifying, and their stocks were clearing faster than expected.

Suddenly, the Messenger barged into the room. "Sir! Sir! It's everywhere! It's on Jwitter, Winstagram!! We're live on ANN now!!"

"What? What's going on …?" asked Govind, CEO of the WILD Company, irritated by the interruption but sensing that something was amiss.

"Switch on the television! The TV … get it on!" shouted The Messenger.

A hush fell on the room as the voice of the newsreader came on. "We bring you breaking news from Animal News Network, outside the City Hospital. Sirens are screeching, ambulances are rushing to the hospital in double-quick time. Paramedics are scrambling to bring trolley-loads of animals into the Emergency Department of the hospital. Our reporter, Rey, is on the scene right now. Rey? What have you found out?"

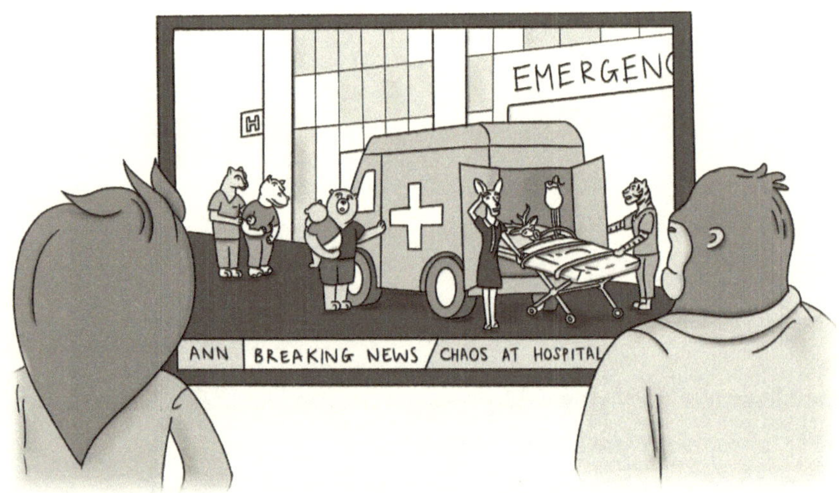

"It's chaos here at the City Hospital," said Rey. "I've not seen such pandemonium in my history as a reporter. I spoke earlier to a tiger who was rushing into the hospital and was told that his cub just suddenly had terrible diarrhoea and vomiting, and his body was burning up. Oh my, look! Here's another ambulance! The paramedics are rolling out an animal—what is it? It's a deer, with drips attached. He looks so pale and is writhing all over, like he's in terrible pain! Let me try to talk with the doe who is accompanying him."

"Excuse me, excuse me, can you tell me what happened to him?" asked the reporter. The frazzled doe looked really scared as she spoke into the microphone, "It was really strange. One moment we were having a lovely meal—we were celebrating our baby's birthday with all our favourite foods—and the next thing you know, my poor, poor Jun fainted and fell to the ground—just like that! Sorry, I've got to go!" With that, the doe rushed into the hospital to look for her loved one.

The reporter continued. "Earlier, I managed to speak with Dr Cheng, Medical Director of the City Hospital, who told me that they were seeing an unprecedented number of animals at the Emergency Department over the past twenty-four hours. Preliminary observations seem to indicate that the torrent of animals are coming in around mealtimes, and it seems that they all had these terrible pains and discomfort immediately after their meal. All the animals I spoke with mentioned the foods they were eating just prior to falling ill. The names of two products cropped up often: AniBurg and SunnyMeal. At the moment, there is no confirmation that these products caused so many animals to fall seriously ill and seek treatment at the hospital. Regardless, all these emergency cases are causing a nightmare for the staff at City Hospital as they are not prepared for a deluge of patients within such a short period of time. Back to you at the studio."

The newsreader continued to speak and this time the images of the WILD and NEON companies showed up on the television screen. "As our reporter mentioned, it seems that all the animals either had a meal of AniBurg or SunnyMeal just before falling ill. These ready-to-eat meals are popular in the community, amongst both the young and old, as they are known to be nutritious and delicious. AniBurg is manufactured by the WILD Company while SunnyMeal comes from the NEON Company. We have reporters now at the Headquarters of WILD and NEON and will be waiting for an opportunity to speak with the executives. Coming up next, we will be speaking with Dr Cheng, Medical Director of City Hospital, whom we managed to interview earlier this morning."

Images of the WILD and NEON company buildings appeared on screen next, with some pictures of the Senior Executives—Chung, CEO of NEON, a third generation tiger in a family business owned and run by tigers, and Govind, CEO of WILD which is a medium-sized enterprise comprising a diverse group of animals—lions, antelopes, bears, tigers, doves, among others.

In the ensuing news segments, reporters questioned the quality of AniBurg and SunnyMeal, as at least two hundred animals had been hospitalised; and the number was rising. Dr Cheng mentioned that the symptoms shown by the animals seemed to indicate that they were suffering from a form of plague and if they had all eaten one of these two products, a conclusion could be that there was some contamination during the production process, as both these companies used a common ingredient.

A loud roar came from Chung, CEO of NEON, as he slammed down the phone in anger. "THAT'S NOT TRUE! TELL ME, THIS IS NOT HAPPENING! SHEN! Come here this instant!"

Shen, Chung's Chief of Staff, came in looking nervous. "Why? What happened, Chung?"

"I just got off the phone with the police! They are coming here, to our office, in thirty minutes!" Chung growled angrily, legs akimbo, looking like he was going in for the kill.

Bewilderment and fear flashed through Shen and she felt the rumblings of something akin to panic. "What? Why? What did we do wrong?"

Chung, getting angrier by the minute at Shen's state of panic, lashed out at her, hissing loudly, "I have told you a million times, and you never listen, never did anything. You did not listen to my instructions. I told you: do not change the supplier, do not use that good-for-nothing company. And you see now what has happened? SunnyMeal was found to have caused all those animals to fall ill."

"But …" Shen started to speak but realised that this was probably not the wisest thing to do, so muttered under her breath, "But, Chung … you ordered us to change suppliers!"

Not missing a beat, Chung continued with his tirade whilst pacing his office. "Why are you standing there? GET THE FOOLS IN HERE! SOMEONE WILL GO TO THE GALLOWS FOR THIS!!!"

Meanwhile, at the WILD Company, the televisions in the canteen, along the main hallways, and in the Council Room where the SET was meeting, were showing the television interview with Dr Cheng. All eyes and ears were glued to the TV screens. It was like all hell had broken loose. Every employee looked shocked and worried. Some started to feel nauseous.

After a moment of silence where every animal tried to make sense of what they saw on the news, Govind, a silverback gorilla, said in a calm voice, "I don't know what exactly happened, but of this I'm sure. We are in the news. And from the looks of it, very bad news.

"Firstly, we need to update the Council. Secondly, I want a team set up, pronto, to investigate this situation. And the most important thing—we need to talk with our employees," continued Govind.

Immediately, everyone started putting up their legs, wings, paws to gain Govind's attention.

Lang the lion, VP of Marketing, was the first to speak up. "I'll take charge of the investigation and set up a cross-functional task force immediately to find out what happened, assess what is the cause, who did it, when it happened."

Olive the orangutan, VP of Operations, followed, "I will work with Lang on this."

The dove, Dhia, who was the VP of Animal and Culture, fluttered her feathers and cooed, "I will draft a statement for you to deliver to all the employees, Govind. We will have to do this immediately as everyone would have heard the news by now." Govind nodded gravely in affirmation.

Aang the antelope, VP of Sales, jumped in. "I stand by our processes. We've been working on improving them over the years. Our manufacturing processes are the best. Something must have happened and I will join Lang's team to investigate and find the root cause."

Lang nodded happily. "I believe I've got my team, Govind. We will report back to you regularly on this. Let's get to work, team!"

The animals started to leave the room quickly, the sense of urgency strong and the commitment to find the root cause clear in everyone's minds.

Left behind were Govind, Rahman the rhinoceros, who was General Counsel, and Bao the brown bear, VP of Finance. "Guys," said Govind, "let's connect with the Council now. Then let me speak with the employees. The police are coming in thirty minutes. We need to get to the bottom of this."

AFTERMATH

Immediately after leaving the Council Room, Lang, Olive, and Aang met to plan their strategy to investigate what caused the crisis. The supplier of the raw materials was invited to be part of the investigation team. One of the first actions was a total recall of all AniBurg products. They were immediately taken off the shelves and the contents sent to the laboratories for analysis. Interviews with staff involved in the supply chain processes started almost immediately and the services of external auditors were secured to audit the entire supply chain processes.

At NEON, however, the situation got into a worsening state of disarray. When CEO Chung held his emergency leadership meeting, paws were pointed in every direction, every leader denied any wrongdoing, and when questioned by police, they seemed completely unaware of the processes they had in place. Each tiger had a theory that the other head of function was to blame.

Every meeting the leadership team had ended up in a blaming exercise—banging of tables, roaring and growling which could be heard down the hallways of the company, and even some rather bloody fights. The

Head of Operations was heard to say that everything and everyone in her function followed the required processes and it was actually Procurement at fault. Even Finance was blamed because the budget requested for was not approved and they had to opt for a cheaper provider. Chung joined in too, and during one particular press interview, declared that there was nothing wrong with SunnyMeal and that AniBurg was the one that caused the plague.

Results of the investigations done by the WILD task force were shared with the police. The conclusion was that the security of the warehouses owned by the supplier was not good enough, and the containers where the raw materials were kept were not well sealed. It was confirmed that this supplier produced the raw materials for both WILD and NEON companies.

With Govind at the helm and strongly supported by his leadership team, the WILD Company managed to recoup and recover some of the bad press they faced when the situation hit them. Govind personally visited patients in hospitals and homes, provided for families, and made sure that they did not want for anything whilst their loved ones were recovering.

In contrast to the activities at the WILD Company, nothing changed at NEON. Sales dropped drastically. SunnyMeal was not taken off the shelves. But no animal was brave enough to buy them for their family, nor any of the other NEON products, especially when they saw the media interview with Chung claiming that there was nothing wrong with SunnyMeal.

Three months later, the police investigations concluded. The culprits turned out to be employees from a rival company that managed to engage some snakes to carry out the heinous task of injecting poisonous substances into the raw materials owned by the supplier. What was originally thought to be the plague turned out to be a very severe case of food poisoning. No new cases of food poisoning linked to these two food items were seen in the City Hospital after that. And it was fortunate that none of those affected suffered badly and eventually all patients recovered, though some took longer than others.

Although the WILD Company suffered some losses during the months following the incident, they managed to secure the confidence of the public that all their other products were safe. At the NEON Company, CEO Chung and the entire leadership team were sacked for not taking accountability and responsibility. But it was too late. The damage was done.

Six months later, Govind and Lang—who had been friends since childhood—were taking a leisurely stroll towards their favourite place, far away from prying eyes and ears.

"Sighhhhh … all's well that ends well. It's just like old times, isn't it, Govind?" said Lang.

"What do you mean, Lang? You used to be such a fire brand … more like that Chung from NEON," countered Govind with a half smile.

"Huh? What do you mean? I'm always the calm, cool, and collected one. You were the angsty one, jumping up and down, and screeching all over the place," teased Lang.

"Oh yeah? You, of all animals, have one of the shortest memories. You've forgotten what happened two years ago, how we all worked hard together to build what we have now? I'm so proud of our achievements. And you did well, Lang," Govind said, with pride in his voice.

Lang, looking immensely pleased and relaxed, drawled, "Well, what can I say? It's all to do with excellent deployment, isn't it, Govind? With decisiveness, discipline, determination, and dedication … *we* did it!"

"Yeah, we did it," Govind acknowledged. "We were in the flow, like one united team, weren't we? And how we worked with the police. Imagine them wanting to find out what our secret formula was! But we couldn't have done it two years ago, could we?"

"Huh, no way! We would have been exactly like NEON," said Lang with a chuckle. "That was a long time ago, wasn't it? How things have changed."

"Indeed! Hey, what do you think? Maybe we could offer to share how we built our culture with the new NEON leadership team. What do you think, Lang?" Govind said excitedly.

"Wow, that's a wonderful idea. Shall we have an Aniburg meal with them?" wondered Lang out loud.

And with that they started to walk home, back to their families, smiling and relaxed, clearly two animals who have gone through thick and thin together.

So, what were things like at the WILD Company two years ago?

A few years earlier ...

02
MAYHEM

CRRAACK!! With a loud roar that reverberated through the corridors of power at the WILD Company, Lang pounded his paws onto the beautifully designed and lacquered kiaat table in the Council Room, breaking it in half. Clearly furious by the proceedings of the Council Meeting, where all accusing eyes were turned on him, Lang stood up and roared, "THIS IS NOT MY FAULT!"

Immediately, a hush enveloped the Council Room. Everyone—Council members, SET members, and other support staff—was taken aback by this sudden loud outburst from Lang.

Eventually, the quiet and calm voice of Osman the Wise, a Verreaux's eagle owl, came through the silence. "If this is not your fault, Lang, who then should take responsibility for this situation that we are now in?"

An even louder roar came from the young lion. In an angry booming voice, Lang spoke, "Why are you asking me this question? Why are you pointing your … your … talons at me? Why is it me? Why me? Why not ask someone else? Why not Hugo? He was leading this project. Or him … and him … and him …" Lang pointed angrily at the others in the room, all of whom were now busy looking down at the ground and not making a sound. "They too were involved. They made a mess of this. Look at what he did! What she did!" Without missing a beat, Lang went on. "They all had a role to play in this, especially Hugo! He was the main contact with our vendors! You should get him to explain what happened, what he did wrong. Why point your talons … paws … whatever at me? They were responsible too. And … and …"

"BE QUIET, LANG!!" Liu roared at the other end of the table that was left standing precariously on one leg. "Be a lion and own up to the mistake you made!"

"Father, you too?" gasped Lang. "What's happening here? Why is it my fault? What did I do wrong? … Govind? Where do you stand on this?"

One look at Govind and Lang knew that all was lost. That riled him even more and he just went ballistic.

"So, none of you are on my side … even you, who consider yourselves my pals, my mates. You are not supporting me. None of you even bothered to listen to my side of the story ... and you've already made up your minds!" Breathing heavily, Lang went on, "FINE! I'm leaving! ... I don't want to be part of this ... this ... atrocity! All of you ... you ... you ..." and with another deafening roar, Lang left the Council Room, bringing down the door with a loud noise—CRAAASH!!—echoing through the hallways.

Everyone in the room fell silent. No one dared move or speak. Realising that everyone needed some breathing space, Eisha, the only elephant in the room, got up from her seat and said, "Right, everyone. Let's take a break. The air in here is too hot for me to handle." Flapping her large ears vigorously, she continued, "All Council Members are to return to this room in five minutes. You, too, Liu ... don't go slinking away!" Eisha had noticed Liu quietly moving towards the hole in the room where the door once stood. "Everyone else, go back to your desks and finish your tasks for the day."

Pacing up and down the corridor, consumed with anger yet worried about the situation they were now in, Liu was livid. "What a mess we have in our paws right now!"

"Work should be easy and fun if you are the boss," Liu fumed. "Sigh, I am indeed getting on in years." Liu had taken over the leadership of this company from his father many years back. And when he retires, it will be Lang's turn to lead. The WILD Company had always been in the lion pride. Helmed by lions and their descendants ... until his grandfather decided to diversify and brought in the giraffes, followed by the silverback gorillas, tigers, leopards, and many other animals. Now it was like a zoo. All the animals working together so closely—lions and giraffes next to peafowl and orangutans! Completely unimaginable, but this was how things were changing around here.

"It's nice that we have the tigers to do the menial tasks but it's not the same as before ... and I definitely do not trust the leopards," Liu thought whilst pacing up and down the hallway. He liked to put his paw into every pie … just like his father and his grandfather before him. He never fully trusted the hyenas and always kept a watchful eye on them because they were up to no good. The silverback gorillas, however, were very straightforward and delivered well—always got things done. "Although I never quite understood their funny accents, their hooting, and the beating of their chests. Why can't they just growl like us lions? Govind is terrific though. He gets along well with Lang and together they have helped build the company to where it is today—strong and feared by others. Our competitors will never be able to catch up. And by the time they do, we will already be several thousand watering holes ahead of the nearest one."

With so much diversity in place, biases and different ways of working had filtered into the organisation over the years causing acrimony and mistrust across the various functions. When Liu's grandfather hired other animals to lead some of the teams in the WILD Company, the lions had to change and adapt pretty quickly. From being the leaders or the know-it-alls, they were now being led by animals other than lions—gorillas, bears, zebras, tigers—who were at times better, smarter, and more effective than the lions in some areas of work. Their egos were hurt; they felt ridiculed at times, which resulted in them not sharing their knowledge and history with the other animals, termed "the new blood" by the lions.

The new blood gave great value and did a lot to help build a successful organisation; but without the deep historical knowledge of how things worked, started to do things their own way, creating new cultures and ways of working within their own teams. Eventually, every team started to create and protect their own turf and built silos. Much mistrust occurred. Animals were not willing to share, did double-work as nobody was talking to each other and not aware of what the other was doing. Team meetings became a mere formality. Even though the company continued to grow, the culture became quite toxic with everyone fighting to take credit when successes were achieved. However, when failures or crises happened, all "fingers" were pointed in directions other than their own.

Liu tried really hard to bring the teams together; but by the time he took over, the toxic culture had been entrenched. And it was too much hard work to do things differently. In fact, it would take a tornado to change the culture of this organisation. "If it ain't broke, don't fix it" was Liu's motto. So as CEO, what Liu did was what his father had done—had separate meetings with each of the leaders, gave them directions as needed, tried to get them to work together but failing miserably in the process. Too much accumulated anger and distrust had been built up over the years.

Despite all this, Liu still managed to lead the diverse organisation, with a strong paw and a loud roar. "Everyone is respectful of me and my leadership of WILD. Perhaps a bit fearful but that's how things are done around here," mumbled Liu under his breath. "And Lang ... I taught him well. He's definitely his father's son."

Ahhh Lang ... Liu's favourite son was well in line to succeed him as CEO. Lang was a star, a high performer, confident, and a risk-taker. Short-tempered and impatient, he had had his fair share of trouble. "But somehow he never really put his paw into every pie like me," reflected Liu thoughtfully. "He likes the easy way out, and always delegates his tasks. His best friend and trusted soulmate, Govind, had always been there to help clear up any mess that he leaves behind."

Govind was his parents' pride and joy. And he was a reflection of all they taught him to be—brave, valiant, courageous, trustworthy, respectful, and honourable. A quiet giant who was a role model in living and behaving like a true warrior. He had been in the WILD Company since graduation and had grown and developed very well. "Pity he's not a lion. But he has been appointed as the second in line to succeed me, after Lang. Which would probably never happen anyway," thought Liu, when the Council chose Govind as second in line to the "throne".

Bringing himself back into the current state of affairs, Liu had realised for some time that the WILD Company was in danger of losing its competitive edge. He had put Lang in charge to devise plans to turn the company around. After all, Lang was in charge of Marketing and Business Development. He had the skills and know-how to look for new business deals. What seemed a good decision at that time turned out to be one of the biggest mistakes Liu made.

One by one, Lang's team of business development experts tendered their resignation. The reason they gave Dhia, VP of Animal and Culture, was that Lang was too difficult to work with. His temper was legendary. He growled and roared whenever things did not go his way. He did not listen, nor did he support the team when they needed help. He just threw them into the deep end and left them there. At the same time, their competitor NEON was hiring aggressively, with better titles and pay.

Even their customers left the WILD Company, choosing instead to work with NEON. NEON had a very friendly and generous VP of Business Development. The complete opposite of Lang in character and behaviour.

Within five minutes, the Council Members returned.

"Right, let's call this meeting to order!" said Osman, the Council Chair, as he flew onto the half of the table that still looked slightly more stable than the other half, which was lying miserably on the floor. Looking foreboding and authoritative, Osman's head moved 180 degrees to where Liu was sitting. In a low commanding voice, he said, "Liu, I'm not happy with Lang's behaviour. I can forgive him for many things, after all I'm his godfather. But to show his temper at a Council Meeting and deny all responsibility is completely unacceptable."

A huge rumble came from what seemed to be the depths of Liu's digestive system that was frighteningly close to becoming a roar, but at the very last minute turned into a loud sigh. "I am not happy with that either, Osman," said Liu. "But he's so good in so many other ways. Look, didn't he bring in that large deal the other day …"

"We're not talking about his ability to deliver on the tasks, Liu. You know that. Lang has completely zero awareness of how bad his behaviour is. And because of that, we have lost our competitive edge." Osman looked at Liu in exasperation.

Another rumble-sigh came out of Liu.

Osman continued, "So, we have two issues that we need to resolve here—the crisis the company is in, and Lang. I really would have liked to have just one issue to resolve but time is not on our side."

Eisha chipped in. "It was really good that all of us witnessed Lang in action, his true colours. Imagine if we appointed him CEO when you retire, Liu, and he did this to us. Where would we all be? Back in the jungle hunting and killing each other? Like in the old days?"

"Growwwlll …" Liu looked ready to pounce on Eisha.

Osman decided to step in. "Now, now, let's focus, everyone. Here's my view. It's no use talking about what happened; that's already history. Let's focus now on the issues we have before us. As far as I can see, we need someone to lead this situation to resolution. We had initially thought it was going to be an easy task for Lang to resolve …"

Osman couldn't finish his sentence as every animal started chiming in at once.

"I don't believe Lang can resolve the situation at all!" said one of the Council Members.

"He will cause an even greater disaster to happen!" another voice chimed in.

"Lang's history," drawled Eisha, swishing her trunk.

Once again, Osman flew to the middle of the room. "Right, everyone, let's stop this nonsense!"

"I believe there is agreement from everyone in this room, including YOU, Liu, that Lang is not the right leader to manage this situation or the right animal to lead WILD. All in agreement raise your right wing, trunk, whatever and say aye."

Osman turned his head 200 degrees across the room, looking sternly at every animal. Quietly and confidently, every animal raised his or her trunk, wing, paw, or hoof and uttered "aye". His eyes settled on Liu. In his deepest tone of voice, Osman said, "We are waiting for you, Liu."

Liu grudgingly raised his paw and growled, "Aye."

"Ahh … we are all in agreement," said Osman. A sigh of relief went through the room.

In a soft voice, Eisha hesitatingly started to speak. "So, shall we nominate another leader to lead this? Perhaps someone who has not been involved in this mess we are in?" Looking around and seeing that everyone was all ears, she continued, "Someone who is calm, and always gives a different view, is able to command yet has the respect of all. Now, who would that be?"

Immediately a quiet voice chimed in "I propose we get Govind to lead. After all, he is our second choice for CEO. We can test him out now. If he succeeds, he will lead our company when Liu retires. If he fails …"

A heavy silence followed.

Osman immediately acted upon the silence and said, "Everyone in favour of the proposal for Govind to take the lead and get us out of this situation, rai—"

"Aye!" "Aye!" "Aye!" "Aye!" "Aye!" Loud and clear, all members of the Council gave their approval to the proposal for Govind to lead the company out of the crisis.

And so it came to be that, for the first time in the history of WILD, the incoming CEO was not a lion. Every animal in the room took a moment to grasp this and let the reality sink in. There was no other candidate. All the other lions were too young and Govind had proven his worth and capability.

After all he was almost a lion, spending most of his childhood years with Lang and they are best mates. With a heavy heart, Liu accepted the decision of the Council and gave his stamp of approval for Govind to lead.

"Right. So who is going to talk with Govind to set this in motion?" Eisha asked.

"I will do so," said Osman. "And I will speak with Lang too. After all, I have been part of their upbringing and growth all these years."

03

THE THREE CONVERSATIONS

OSMAN AND LANG

Osman found Lang seated at what was left of a desk, all scratched up and in pieces. Osman thought: "If this desk had been in any way alive, I bet it suffered the most slow and painful death ever." Settling his feathers slowly and facing Lang, Osman said softly, "That was completely out of character, Lang. You are no longer a lion cub. Whatever made you burst out like that, and at the Council Meeting too?"

Not liking the tone of Osman's voice and shaking his head in bewilderment, Lang replied, "What do you mean? Were you deaf? Did you not hear the way that Eisha grilled me with so many accusations? It was as if I was the one who caused this situation to happen. I've already been judged guilty by everyone in that room! I was not given a chance to explain!" With a sharp intake of breath, Lang continued, "Did you all not give your blessings for this initiative from the very beginning? And did you all not hand me Hugo to work with? And no one, none of you, helped me out. None of you even said a word on my behalf. It was as if I was sent to the slaughter, guilty without being given any chance to prove my innocence." The words came out at machine-gun speed, causing Lang to choke and cough.

"No … no … no …" Osman held up his wing to stop Lang from continuing to speak. "Again, let me say this. It is completely out of character for someone who was in line to succeed the leadership of this company to behave in this way."

Lang's head jerked up in disbelief. "Wh-wh-what do you mean? Wh-what are you saying, Osman? Was in line?" The words just could not come out from his mouth. Never before had Lang been so frightened. Never in his entire life had he felt so alone. It felt as if his whole world was crashing down around him. He felt himself shaking from the top of his head all the way through to his tail.

A huge sigh came from the depths of Osman's innards. "I'm old, Lang … and I'm not good at these things, but … Lang, irrespective of whether you are innocent or otherwise, there are a few things that we expect of a CEO or his successor. Your behaviour at the Council Meeting earlier today …" Osman heaved an even bigger sigh. Squaring his shoulders, Osman said, "The Council made their decision today. Govind will be succeeding your father, Liu, as CEO of the WILD Company."

"Noooooooo!!" With a strangled roar, Lang ran wildly out of the building and into the jungle, demolishing anything that came into his path.

"SIGHHH …" Osman looked dejectedly at the fast-disappearing Lang. "I'll wait a few more days to talk with him again. I don't want him to do anything hasty. Let me talk with Govind. Perhaps he can calm Lang down a bit. Although I'm not so sure if Govind will be able to be of any help. SIGHHH …" With that, Osman flew to where Govind was busy trying to help the team work to salvage the situation on the ground.

OSMAN AND GOVIND

"Govind! Govind!" Osman screeched from a distance.

Just as Govind raised his head, Osman came swooping down, his wing almost clipping Govind's ear in the process. "Hey, Osman, that was a bit close! What's all the excitement about?"

"Ohhh, my poor heart …. Let me catch my breath first, Govind," Osman said.

"All ears now …" Govind stood up straight on his two hind legs and patiently waited for Osman to compose himself.

"Right, Govind," Osman started … and then stopped. "No, I can't do this. He's much taller than I, and I want to be able to see his eyes," thought Osman. So, instead he said, "Come, come, let's go over to the waterfall. Over there, by the sycamore tree. It can give us some shade as well as let us talk comfortably."

Really curious now, Govind followed Osman as they made their way to the tree in silence.

Osman started again. "Right, Govind …" he said as he jumped on a rock and looked at Govind squarely in the eye. "Yes, Osman?" responded Govind politely.

Suddenly feeling uncomfortable, Osman started ruffling his feathers and flapping his wings, unable to maintain eye contact with Govind. "I want to give you an update on our discussion at the Council Meeting after, you know, the incident …"

"Yes?" Govind said whilst holding his breath. "Do continue, Osman," he said politely and patiently.

"Well … ahhh … as you know, Lang went completely overboard at the Council Meeting," Osman started.

"He was … angry …" Govind tried valiantly to protect his friend.

"Well, yes … and you know he's never been able to control his temper," Osman's voice was getting a pitch higher now.

Arms akimbo, Govind spoke, the words coming out slowly and clearly, "Well, you guys were rather mean to him. None of you gave him a chance to explain. I felt that he was already pronounced guilty by every animal in that room …"

"Including you …" Osman interjected.

"Yesss, including me …" sighed Govind. "I didn't give him my support this time round."

Osman knew he got Govind where he wanted. "Exactly Govind! You've always had his back at those Council Meetings. Lang always got his way because you supported him, all the time."

Confused with why Osman was bringing this up, Govind looked straight into Osman's eyes and asked, "What are you trying to say, Osman?"

"What I'm saying, Govind, is that Lang always counted on you to support him and you gave him your all. But this time, his temper got the better of him—and in front of the Council too. So Lang showed his true colours … his lack of awareness, his lack of leadership—of himself and of the situation."

"Wait … what are you trying to say?" Govind asked incredulously.

"Sighhh … Govind, we know both of you so well. Lang would make some mess and you would clear it up for him. And you always did it so well, all the time, that the Council never made a fuss. After all, Lang was going to succeed Liu. You two are best buddies. More importantly, none of the 'misdeeds' ever hurt the WILD Company. But now this thing. We are losing profits, we are losing staff. Nobody wants to join our company. Dhia is tearing her feathers out because NEON has managed to poach our employees—our stars and our talents. This is not good, Govind. And for the first time ever, we saw Lang just 'losing it' … and he really failed to show his leadership." Osman let out another deep sigh.

"Errr … say that again, Osman. What do you mean about Lang 'losing it'? Losing what?" Govind asked, bewildered by what Osman was saying.

"We need to resolve this issue, Govind. And we need to do this soon. You are the only one we trust to lead us out of this mess," Osman continued.

"Yeah, I will do this for sure. You can count on me, as always," Govind quickly responded, trying hard to understand what Osman was getting to.

"Well, yes. Not only that, Govind. The Council has decided … and this was a unanimous decision …" Osman took a deep breath, squared his shoulders and said, "We have decided that Lang will not be in line to succeed Liu as CEO."

"Whaaa …? Say that again …" Caught completely off guard, Govind just stared at Osman, his mouth open and his hackles starting to rise. He was completely shocked with what he just heard Osman say and slowly getting absolutely worried and concerned.

Everything seemed so quiet and peaceful except for some cicadas chirping away in the summer heat. But Govind could feel and hear his heart pounding heavily in his chest. "Unfortunately, after the incident in the Council Room today, we all agreed that Lang is no longer first in line to succeed Liu … and the leader we assign to lead us out of the mess will take over as first in line to be the next CEO. That would be you …" Osman placed his wing tip onto Govind's heart as he repeated, "You, Govind. You are now the WILD Company's first choice to take over as the next CEO when Liu retires."

Stunned into silence, Govind could only stare at Osman. Looking into his eyes, he knew that Osman was not joking, not that he ever did.

Govind felt shivers going down his spine … and the only thought he had was Lang—had he been informed? How was he going to take this?

Reading Govind's mind, Osman sighed again. "Lang was told … just now."

Govind blinked. Then everything came rushing out, in a louder voice than Govind intended, "What do you mean 'Lang was told'? You just 'told' him your decision? How could this happen? Do you realise what you've done? You could have done better, Osman, and engaged Lang in a better way. What a mess! What a mess! I need to talk with Lang … I need to find him! How can you all do this to him? Do you know what the consequences are? You, of all the … the … animals in our homeland!" Govind went down on all fours and turned to run … but then, just as quickly, he stopped in his tracks and looked at Osman. "Wait, wait … is this decision final? Can it be rescinded?"

"Time for me to go, Govind," and with that, Osman flew away.

LANG AND GOVIND

Govind knew where he could find Lang. It was their sacred space—a safe space for them to talk, plan pranks, and while away the time, hiding from the adults, especially when they knew they would get punished. They continued to use this place when they got older—just talking, playing, having fun, sometimes just doing nothing.

Whenever Lang got angry or upset, he would go into a rampage and tear down everything in his path. Eventually tired out, he would go to their hiding place—deep in the jungle, by the rock, near the lake—to calm down. He would hide there, get really mad with the world until he wore himself out and fell asleep. In the morning, everything would be over.

When Govind found Lang, he realised that this was not the normal situation. Lang was still madly pacing and breaking everything apart—the branches and rocks that they had both painstakingly put in place so that no animal would ever think there was a comfortable hiding place there. The whole place was such a mess that Govind doubted they would ever be able to clear it up.

Lang was growling and whimpering at the same time.

"He really looks like he is in deep pain," thought Govind.

Lang raised his head upon hearing some noise. "Well, well, well, what do you know? The new CEO is here to punish me."

Seated on the ground, Govind just kept quiet, knowing that this was not the time to talk and giving Lang time to blow off steam and whatever was on his chest.

"Say something!!" Lang roared as he paced up and down while staring angrily at Govind.

Govind said quietly, "We need to get to the bottom of this, Lang. We have to initiate an investigation. You need to tell me what happened."

"Nothing much to tell. Hugo told me everything was good. And I believed him …" Lang said in an exasperated manner. "And why shouldn't I believe him and let him take the lead? After all, he's supposed to be the best ever, isn't he? That's what Father said. Dhia never challenged that. Don't you recall Father saying that Hugo is the best for this role, hinting to me that I wasn't good enough? Since he is the best and I'm not, why should I interfere? After all, Father brought him in. I had nothing to do with this. I had no choice in this matter at all …"

"Clearly, Lang is in a foul mood and still very defensive of his actions," thought Govind, as he continued to let Lang rave and rant away.

"That Council Meeting … that topped it all. How the topic suddenly changed and every single animal in there pointed all their wily digits at me! That really made me so mad! Where was Hugo? Why wasn't he even at the meeting? Why did I get the blame? This is crazy, absolutely nonsensical. It is not fair! You are all not fair to me!" Lang went on.

Lang glared angrily at Govind, looking despondent yet at the same time trying to be the brave lion that he is. "I don't know. I guess when everyone was just staring at me as if I was at fault, it just got to me. And when I looked at you, and you looked so shocked and startled … I guess I just lost it."

"Yeah, you did," Govind ventured at last.

"I'm still very angry, very mad. I've been working so hard all this time, preparing to become CEO. How can they deprive me of this? For this … this … error that wasn't even my fault! It's just not fair!!! How can they arrive at this decision? Lions have always been the CEO of the WILD Company. How can they let another animal who's not a lion lead this company?

"What a disaster it will be for us all! I have completely lost face in front of the whole lion pride! And the animal kingdom to boot! Imagine a gorilla leading the WILD Company! ARRHHH!" Lang roared in frustration … then suddenly stopped, realising that the animal that was not a lion who was chosen to lead the WILD Company, was standing just a few metres away from him.

Realising his mistake, he tried to make amends, although half-heartedly. "But if I'm not destined to be CEO, then the next best animal to lead the WILD Company would be you. But it's still extremely unfair. I'm still angry. But I can't hate you … No! No, I can't … as much as I want to …" Lang muttered, shaking his mane in frustration and anger.

As Lang was about to go into another tirade, Govind jumped in. "This is not going anywhere, Lang. A decision has been made. So let's abide by that for the time being. You never know when things may change. For now, I need your help, Lang."

Confused, Lang looked at Govind. The gorilla continued, "I've been asked to lead a team to investigate the situation we are now in, to propose a solution and effectively deploy a new way to bring our company back on its feet again. I need your help on this. But I can't have you getting crazily angry again. Will you promise to help with this?"

"Yeah, yeah," Lang said, "Now leave me alone. I am tired …"

Knowing that there was no point in continuing this conversation with Lang now, Govind left.

04
REFLECTIONS AND ACTIONS

GOVIND TAKES CHARGE

Having had some time to think through the conversations he had with Osman and Lang, Govind had many thoughts running through his mind, foremost of which was, "This can't really be true! The WILD Company has always been under the stewardship of the lion pride. Why would a small mistake from Lang, and primarily from a behavioural perspective, make the Council decide otherwise?"

But Govind had more urgent and important tasks at hand so he decided to put aside the thought about him being CEO for the moment. He needed to work out a plan to present to the Council on how he was going to turn the company around. "The SET meeting is tomorrow and I have to present my plan to resolve this situation then. I need a team in place to work on this, together. Where can I find the right animals? Do we even have these talents?"

"Let me find Liu. I need his support …"

GOVIND AND LIU

Liu was not in a good mood at all. His reputation was in tatters. The shares of the WILD Company were down. There were rumours that the Council would call for his early retirement. On top of this, his succession plans had been put in disarray. His favourite son was no longer going to be crowned the next king of the WILD Company. Lang managed to destroy the leadership lineage of the lions. A silverback gorilla—a gorilla, a primate not a lion—was going to lead the company. What a nightmare!

Govind found Liu seated in his office, looking miserable and old.

"Liu …" Govind started. Liu did not move at all. "Liu …" Govind repeated, slightly louder this time. "Look, Liu, Lang's my best friend, my mate. I don't wish to hurt him at all. And never in my wildest dream would I do anything that would destroy our friendship. From the time we joined the WILD Company, you'd made it clear to everyone that he's going to take over from you. I totally respect that and I expect that to happen one day. It doesn't make sense to me that I would take over as the next CEO. I don't really want the CEO job. I don't really care about it at all. Right now, all I care about is to focus on how to resolve this situation that we are in."

Liu looked up at Govind, startled by what he had just heard. Looking into Govind's eyes, Liu realised that this young gorilla was indeed telling the truth. He felt slightly better and wanted to respond … but words could not come out.

Govind took Liu's silence as an acknowledgement of what he had said and continued, "I plan to set up a team to deliver on the Council's demands. I cannot do this alone. And time is not on our side. So, this is my proposal …"

Liu straightened up. "What is Govind talking about?" he wondered.

Govind continued. "I want every SET member to appoint one member from his or her function to be a member of a Task Force Team I'm setting up. This team's remit will be as follows: investigate the root causes of the issues we are facing—who, why, what, when, how—and then recommend the right solutions for the SET, for the whole WILD Company.

"We've always run our organisation in a top-down, siloed approach. This style of leadership may work for some but not necessarily every function. There is always a winner; but there are also many losers. We need to change how we work. And I would like to do things differently now, to hear from the voices of all our animals ..."

"What do you mean ... set up a team, voice of the animals? What animals? What voice? There is only one voice—and it is the voice from the top echoing across the organisation," Liu was completely astounded and aghast with what Govind had put forward to him. Where on earth did all this come from? It was completely unheard of and it did not seem right. It did not seem logical at all.

Liu started, "Now, now, let's not get all excited here. What are you trying to do here, Govind? For decades, we've had really great work. We've done things in certain ways and they have been working well. Every animal is doing great work at WILD—our investors are happy, our Council is happy ..." Liu stopped abruptly.

One look at Govind and Liu realised he had to change tack. "Don't you agree, Govind, these past years, our profits are healthy, we've beaten our fiercest competitor and we're the top company in the animal world."

Another look from Govind, and Liu compromised. "Okay, okay. Even though we're top by only a really small margin and our profits are slightly down this year ... but look how motivated the animals are ..."

Realising that he was getting himself into a bit of a twist talking about the employees' motivation when the animal turnover rate within WILD was at an all-time high now, Liu tried to get himself out of the corner. "Okay, okay, so you want to try something different. Why not? We're in a bit of a fix right now. But how can you be sure this will work? What makes you confident that this is the only solution we have?"

Govind said, "You are right. Nothing seems to be working now. I'm glad we have the same awareness of the position we are in. We have an opportunity to try something different. Let me say this. Even though we've not tried it before across the organisation, it has worked for me and my team."

Liu looked up sceptically. Govind continued, "Do you remember the SAVE project? The project my team did last year? You saw the numbers, and how we managed to create the much-needed savings to achieve our targets. I had set up a team, and although it was primarily from my function, I did get some help from Bao, as we wanted to know the numbers, and Dhia, who helped facilitate some of the team meetings. Do you remember when Olive presented this to SET and what you said?"

Liu remembered clearly what had happened. "Yeah, I thought for a female, Olive was pretty impressive."

Ignoring Liu's remark, Govind continued, "I remember you saying that Olive could one day succeed me. Coming back to what I was saying. Imagine if we could replicate a similar effort to resolve this situation. What happened that day at the Council Meeting was an explosion, a volcano eruption. It was a blaming contest. Who could fault Lang for being the loudest? Everyone was at their worst. And Lang … you witnessed Lang's helplessness and subsequent tirade. It is not due to incompetence or incapability. Every animal has been trained well to do his or her job. They can handle their responsibilities blindfolded—you know that. You have been involved in their training."

Liu nodded. Taking that as encouragement to continue, Govind said, "It's how we all behave when we're together, how we talk to one another. There is no respect. No one trusts the other. We don't even say 'hello'. No, no, no … we don't even look at each other when we pass in the hallways, or when we see each other by the watering hole. It's as if no one existed except ourself or our tribe."

Govind paused, looking for signs that Liu was not happy, but Liu seemed to be taking in all of what Govind was saying, so he decided to continue. Taking a deep breath, Govind went on, "Do we really care about the WILD Company at all? Where is our loyalty? Why do the animals even want to work here? I know our training is the best in the animal world. We've got so many awards to show for. But if we could all care a little bit more for each other, and for the work we do here, perhaps … perhaps, we would have had each other's back." Govind's voiced trailed off softly. He wasn't quite sure how Liu would take this and waited for a reaction.

Liu realised there was a semblance of truth in what Govind had said. Govind's words showed how much he cared for the company, and the success of the company. It was indeed brave of the young gorilla to say what he did, especially to someone who was part of the company's founding family. The words were so powerful. And what great insights. Liu nodded and said, "So, what's on your mind, Govind?"

"I want to have a team that is forward-looking. Actually, I want animals who are able to work together, despite being from different functions or are different from each other—different cultures and lifestyles, with their diverse views. My dream is to have one united animal team made up of staff who want to work and play together.

"Coming back to the remit that has been given to me. With a one-month timeline to deliver a recommendation, we need to think and work differently. It means we need to create a new way of working together, a new way of talking to each other … a new language to get things done together, a new language to work together.

"The current way of working—where animals do not talk to each other, do not take accountability, where they hide information, do things their own way, repeat the same effort in different functions—will not work. At least not for this team. If I'm tasked to lead this team towards a successful outcome, I want to do things differently. I need to do things differently."

Liu was still unsure about what Govind was saying, but he could not see any other solution or way forward. He recalled the recently completed SAVE project that Govind's function did—they achieved awesome results and saved the company quite a lot of money. Maybe he had a point.

"Go on, I'm listening …" Liu said.

"Firstly, each SET member will recommend one of their star members to this team. The animals in this team must know their functions well. They could either be the leaders themselves or their second-in-command. This team will meet for two days—in fact, I want to meet tomorrow. During this meeting, I want them to be clear on our goal and the outcomes we must achieve together. It would be good for you to join at the start too, so they hear the message from you.

"Following that, we will brainstorm solutions and tasks to be done to achieve the goals, agree on milestones and timelines, assign tasks to everyone, with clear follow-up actions, etc. In addition, this team will meet regularly—and I'm thinking even daily—as we continue to plan, refine our strategy, discuss progress, challenges, and any support that we will need to deliver on our tasks. We may have clear goals and outcomes, but they will decide and agree on how to achieve the outcomes—together—and every team member will be held accountable and responsible for the success that they will achieve as a team."

"Yeeaahh …" drawled Liu, "these are all just words, nice corporate-sounding words. Why do you need to meet for two days? We cannot spare so much time for these animals to be away from their work. What will you be discussing? Sounds to me that you are all just spending time talking and not doing anything. Why not just assign tasks to everyone and get them to do it?"

Patiently, Govind explained, "That's what we've always done—assign tasks and get our staff to do them, and expect that they know exactly what to do, and will deliver accordingly. That's what they do in their daily tasks and assignments. Sometimes not very well either and rarely within the timelines we desire. But the current situation we are in now is not normal. We need every single animal to deliver on their tasks within one month. And we need them to be committed to work with each other. Together, we will achieve more."

Realising the sincerity in Govind's words, Liu said, "I want to be very frank with you, Govind. I really don't follow everything you're saying. I agree the SAVE project team produced some great results. But you were their leader so they would listen and follow your lead. I've always ruled with an iron paw and it worked for me. So doing things different would mean a huge change for the staff. However, my leadership style is perhaps something of the past. As we have a much younger cohort of workers now, that might not work anymore. In addition, I'm willing to give you a chance since this is the Council's decision. Osman probably has seen something that I've not."

"So, what do you need from me? Anything at all?" asked Liu. "It seems like you've got everything worked out." Pleasantly surprised at what Liu said, Govind decided to push on. "Well, not quite. I know for sure that I do not have the expertise to work with a team across the various functions. I would like to get some expert help on this."

"Aaahhh …" said Liu, getting the clarity that he needed now.

Govind continued, "I know of a consultant who has achieved great success in working with teams and I want to bring him in to work with this team. I hear he has worked with ACE Inc., MIB, and some of the big banks too. See how these companies have taken off and grown in their respective industries? For this to happen, I would need some budget. I'm thinking we could utilise what has always been put aside for animal development activities. We don't do anything with it, so, year in and year out, the money just gets put back into the coffers.

"I strongly believe that when we put the right processes in place, things will change for the better. But first things first. Do I have your approval to use the budget, Liu? No extra cost will be needed. We're just using something that's already been set aside and unused every year. We need to do something, Liu, so please help me."

"Okay, I will tell Bao that you have full authority to spend this money, no obstacles, no buts, nothing," said Liu.

"Thank you, Liu! Thank you so much!" Govind said. "And will I get your support when I present to the Council?"

"Yes, yes, of course," said Liu. With that Govind left, energised that he would be able to pull off this massive task in one month.

After Govind left, Liu reflected deeply on the conversation. A thought came to his mind, "If only Lang behaved more like Govind …" Liu decided to look for Lang.

LIU AND LANG

Liu found Lang at the sacred spot, sitting quietly, looking far out into the vast wilderness. He looked lost and sad. Liu thought to himself: "My boy, my pride and joy. What did I do to get him to be in this position now? What have I done? He looks completely destroyed."

"Lang," Liu started.

"Father?" a startled Lang looked up to see his father standing a metre away from him. "I did not hear you coming. What are you doing here?" His father had never come to look for him before. In fact, Lang always received instructions to meet his father. "What's caused this change," wondered Lang.

"I wanted to talk with you, my son," said Liu.

"Oh sure. Please go ahead," Lang mumbled. In his mind, Lang was thinking furiously, "What is he going to talk to me about now? Why did he look for me? What is he going to say? I hope it's not about that incident in the Council Room. Is he going to validate what Osman said to me? I wish I could disappear from here right now ..."

"Ahhh ..." reminisced Liu, "this used to be one of my secret spots, in the old days when I had to hide from my father." He chuckled. "I guess this is your favourite spot too? Looks like some tornado visited recently. Anyway, let me say my piece and then I'll leave." Taking a deep breath, Liu remarked quite strictly, "Firstly, it was completely out of character for you to blow your top the way you did at the Council Meeting."

Lang's tail immediately started swinging from side to side, indicating he was getting angry and was about to talk when Liu stopped him by holding up his right paw. "Hold on and let me finish what I have to say. You were the heir-apparent, a role model, trustworthy and fearless. You should have been in charge of the situation and that would have been the next step for you to be crowned CEO. But you lost it. You got yourself into a corner and you ... lost ... it ... in front of the Council—the very group that would have endorsed you as the next leader of WILD.

"There is no turning back now. The Council's decision is final." Liu let this sink in before continuing. "Govind will now lead the investigation. In a month's time, Govind will present to the Council the results of the investigation, and propose some corrective actions to be deployed across WILD. I do not plan to announce Govind as my successor until he delivers. If he succeeds, he will be crowned. If he fails … maybe, just maybe, there could be an opportunity for you, my son …"

Lang looked up at his father, "What do you mean?"

"If you play your cards right, there could still be an opportunity for you to lead WILD," said Liu, pausing to see Lang's reaction. "For this, you would need to show the Council that you want to change, to improve."

"But there's nothing I need or even want to change about me. I'm perfectly fine with who I am. What's wrong with me being me? And what on earth are you talking about, Father?" Lang said, his tail swinging even faster now.

"Slow down … slow down and listen to me," said Liu. "The Council, especially Osman, has a very healthy respect for Govind and his leadership style. I see that as the only difference between you and him. Both of you are smart. Both of you have worked the same number of years in WILD, both of you have had experience working across functions. All the animals respect you …"

"I'm not so sure about that last bit. But what are you suggesting, Father? Get to the point. I know you are here for a reason, so just get it out," Lang asked.

"Go get yourself a coach." Liu said it so quickly that he wasn't even sure he said it clearly.

"WHAT?" shouted Lang, completely shocked and not at all expecting to hear this from his father.

"Yes, you heard me, Lang. Go get yourself a coach!" Liu said, slower this time and with force. "Go talk to Dhia. Find out where Govind found his coach."

"Why should I get myself a coach?" Lang was confused, trying to link all the dots together on what his father was telling him. "I really don't understand what you are saying. And how do you know that Govind has a coach?" Lang asked.

"I have my sources ..." said Liu.

"But you never believed in this before. I recall Govind saying that you wouldn't sponsor all these mushy stuff, that it's all namby-pamby, touchy-feely whatever, and that nobody in WILD needs it. That you don't see why any animal would even think of getting a coach, especially an executive coach," Lang countered. "And I don't understand why you now believe I need one."

"Yes, I remember that well. But maybe I was wrong. I've been wrong before, and made some mistakes ... some terrible mistakes too.

"I'm getting old, Lang. Things aren't the way they used to be. What I did well when I was young no longer seems to work now. Our new hires are more demanding, more articulate, and they are hungry for promotion, money, and power. When they don't get what they want here, they leave and join our competitors. We need to keep our talent. Govind's team is the only group that has not had a resignation in the past twelve months. He must be doing something right. I'm not sure if you're aware, but they seem to be different compared to the rest—more confident, happier. When they facilitate meetings, the meetings run like clockwork, and decisions are made with clear follow-up actions! The rest of us struggle to even agree on the decision to be made, much less have follow-up actions assigned!"

"Yes, I've seen that. I participated in some of their meetings too. Great discussions and, yes, good outcomes too. So, what would you like me to do, Father?" asked Lang.

"Go talk with Dhia. She'll have some good advice on who would be a good coach for you. Of that I'm very sure ..." said Liu.

SET MEETING

"What a surprise," Liu thought as he looked around the room. Every animal was on time—some were even early!—for this emergency meeting that he had called. Lang, Govind, Rahman, Dhia, Bao and, my goodness, Zack too. Zack was always late! He had never ever been on time for any meeting … or actually for anything. But now, here he was, sitting in the Council Room quietly minding his own business. And it's one minute to the hour when

Organisation Chart

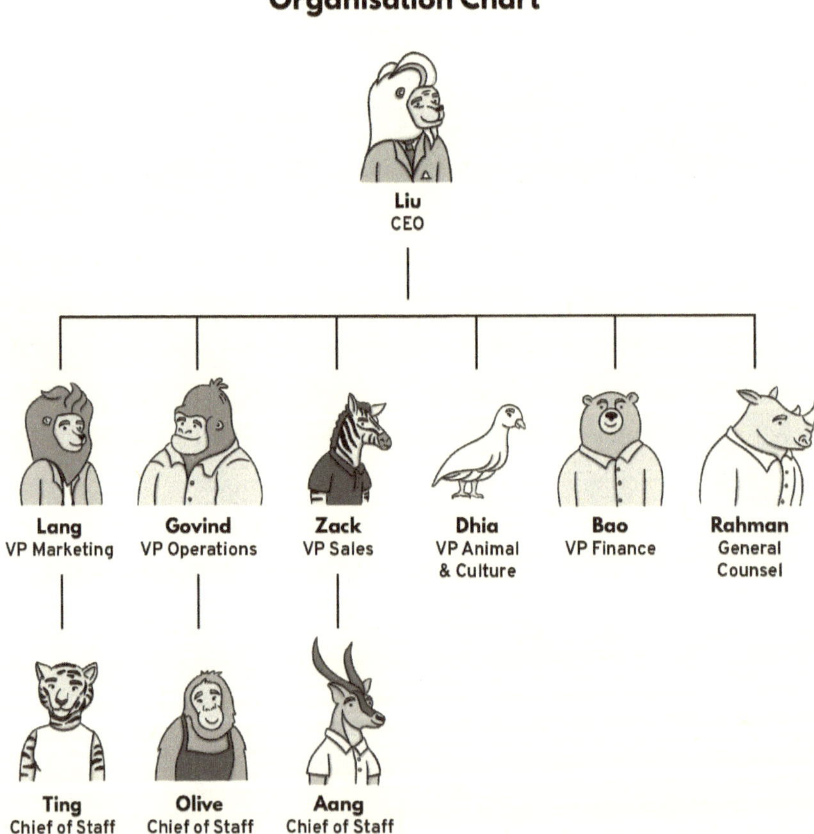

the meeting was supposed to start. "What a surprise!" Liu repeated, under his breath.

Liu had gathered his leadership team together after his talk with Lang. He felt energised, even though it was a difficult time. He knew this was the right thing to do. And so, with a loud tap of his claw on the table, he started to talk.

"The Council wants answers. Our staff wants answers. We want answers. With our key customers threatening to pull out, and our talents leaving us to work for NEON, we need to find answers ... quickly! Who, what, how, when—all these need to be investigated. Following this, I expect some clear recommendations—what needs to be changed, what will the change look like, how will we deploy the changes across the organisation, etc.

"Govind will lead a cross-functional team to work on this. Govind has my support and also that of the Council. I want all of you to support Govind and his team to make sure that we deliver on time, or even earlier.

"If you have no questions, I will hand this meeting over to Govind to walk through his plans with you." With that, Liu sat down and Govind shared his plans with the leaders in the room.

05
AWARENESS

DHIA AND LANG

Although she had never been involved in almost all of the hiring processes at WILD, Dhia, the ring-necked dove, Vice President of Animal and Culture—better known as A&C—function, was no longer unhappy. There was light at the end of the dark tunnel.

Since she joined the WILD Company many years ago, she realised that neither could she influence nor impose on the functional leaders any standard hiring processes, including who they wanted on their teams. The WILD Company had grown from a small organisation of fifty staff to a massive six hundred in just one decade. With the diversity that Liu's father initiated, every animal leader hired their own kind, the ones they trusted, their friends, their friends' friends—the ones they knew would understand their thought processes, and more importantly, take any secrets they might have to their graves. As such, there was never a common set of hiring procedures to follow. Every leader created his or her own hiring process.

Liu was probably the worst. He hired anyone that he felt could be an asset to him and him alone, and ordered—no, commanded—the leaders to take them in. This diversity brought in different cultures and values. Disagreements occurred. Fights happened. Animals got wounded in the process, became disengaged and demotivated. Then they would leave. But they did not leave alone. They brought their friends with them, and headed just around the corner, to their competitors, to NEON and to DUMA Inc.

And even if she had her doubts about any new hire that Liu brought in, there was nothing she could do about it. A roar from him and one of her feathers would drop off! But for sure, Hugo was one of the worst hires ever. He lacked motivation and it showed on his face. He always sneaked off early from work; where he went, no one knew. More importantly, what did Liu see in him? And poor Lang was so fearful of his father that he just took Hugo in and completely ignored what he did. "Was that the right thing to do?" thought Dhia. "Well, it's all too late now. We are in such a mess!"

She cocked her head to one side as the next thought popped into her head: "Perhaps now is the time when change will happen."

Lo and behold, who should appear at the bottom of the tree where Dhia was resting but Lang! "Why is Lang here?" wondered Dhia. "He's never sought me out before. He doesn't even acknowledge my existence!"

"Dhia!" called Lang. "May I speak with you for a minute?"

"Sure thing, Lang." Dhia flew down from the branch she was resting on, to land on a rock nearby. She was now about a metre away from Lang.

"Errr … Dhia … I would like to get your views on something," Lang started.

"Go on. I'm listening," said Dhia.

"Well, this is really odd and I just don't know how best to put it … but Father wanted me to speak with you," ventured Lang.

"Liu? What would Liu want from me?" Dhia fluttered her wings in agitation.

Seeing Dhia agitated made Lang uncomfortable and he started to back away. "There's no way I'm going to talk with Dhia about getting a coach," he thought. "What on earth am I doing here talking with her anyway? I've got better things to do."

"Hang on, Lang." Dhia flew over to Lang as he started walking away. Realising that he was not stopping, Dhia did the only thing she could do. She landed on his head.

"I apologise. The reason I was surprised when you mentioned your father was because I cannot recall when he last spoke with me or even sought me out for anything related to Animal and Culture," said Dhia, balancing herself on Lang's head as he strode off. "So, what is it that Liu wanted you to talk with me about?"

"Well, maybe it's good I can't see you so I can pretend I'm just talking to myself," muttered Lang.

"What's that you're saying, Lang? Could you speak louder? I can't hear you from up here," said Dhia.

"Right, where was I? Okay, here goes." Lang took a deep breath before he continued, "Well, you were at the Council Meeting. And you saw what happened. Next thing I knew, I was ousted and Father tells me that the Council, actually Osman, did not appreciate me getting angry during that meeting." Lang said.

"Well, yes, that's right," said Dhia.

"It's NOT RIGHT! It's downright unfair and incredibly unwarranted!" shouted Lang as he started to swish his tail. Dhia flew off Lang's head to face him directly as she slowly and firmly said, "Well, well, well. If that's not bad behaviour that I'm seeing right now, then what is it?"

"Sigh. Okay, okay. Why is it that I always get angry? I can feel my blood boiling all through my veins when I'm angry. I don't like the way I'm feeling because when it's all over and I'm calm and rational, I realise that I need not be so angry at all. And, of course, by then it's too late. I cannot undo what I said or what I did," said Lang. "And I get angry over the smallest things— when I hear Hugo's footsteps in the corridor, when there's silence in the room, when nobody responds to my questions, even when Father gives me advice …" Lang sounded extremely dejected as he spoke.

Another sigh and this time it seemed to come from the depths of his chest as Lang continued, "What shall I do, Dhia? What can I do?"

"Well, what would you like to see happen, Lang?" asked Dhia as she perched herself on Lang's head again.

Lang started to walk again, talking as he walked. "If I could be more calm … calm like Govind. Well, maybe I can't be exactly like him, but maybe a bit calmer and not get angry over the slightest thing. I've never seen Govind angry with any animal or at any issue ever. Have you seen Govind angry, Dhia?"

Not waiting for Dhia to respond, Lang continued, "Come to think of it, even when we were young, Govind never really got mad. He did get angry but there was always justification for his anger. But it was a controlled anger. And sometimes, I think he faked his anger just to frighten off the other animal. If I could have half of Govind's good nature, that would probably be a good place to start. Do I make sense, Dhia?"

"Completely. And I totally get what you're saying, Lang. May I suggest something? Now, this is just a suggestion—and you have the option to say no. But if you like what I say … well, then perhaps this would be an option for you to consider how you could learn to be half as good natured as Govind," said Dhia.

"Go on, I'm listening," said Lang, walking slower this time to make sure he caught every word that Dhia said.

"Well, I'm thinking that you won't be able to learn how to manage your anger on your own. Perhaps having a coach to work with you on this may help you create the awareness of what your triggers are." As she said the last few words, Dhia got ready to take flight again, in case Lang started moving his tail from side to side. But she was pleasantly surprised that Lang's tail didn't move at all. Instead, he actually stopped walking and sat down!

"Yes, perhaps I do need help, Dhia. Father suggested I speak to you about this actually. And I'm open to seeking help. My anger cost me the CEO job. Because of my anger, I have lost credibility amongst the employees in WILD. I want to change, but I don't know how to. And if a coach can help me change, help me create that awareness you mentioned, I'm willing to give it a shot. What else do I have to lose? I've completely lost face in front of the lion pride," said Lang dejectedly.

Dhia spoke then. "Liu is very wise. You are too, Lang. And I see your sincerity in wanting to change. Let me see how I can help. I know Lana, Govind's coach. She's very good and has many years of experience as an executive coach. I'll seek her advice on what would be the best way forward for you." With that she flew off, but turned back to say, "I'm so happy to have had this conversation with you, Lang. Take care and I'll see you soon!"

DHIA AND GOVIND

Dhia was indeed feeling very positive about the current situation. "Things are moving ahead and perhaps this is when we will see some real changes happening. Talking about changes, I wonder where I can find Govind? I wonder how he's feeling right now?" As these thoughts went through her mind, who did she see in the clearing but Govind himself.

"Hey, Govind!" Dhia called out, fluttering her wings and landing on Govind's wide shoulders. "How are you, Govind?"

Not missing a step, Govind continued moving. "Doing good, Dhia, doing good. A few more loose ends to tie up and I'll be ready for the Council Meeting tomorrow."

"That is really great! You're working at supersonic speed! Can I help in any way, Govind?" ventured Dhia.

"That's awfully kind of you, Dhia. I'll take you up on your offer. It's always good to have an independent view. Are you available now? It would probably take thirty minutes or so. We can go through them in my office. I've got everything in there," said Govind.

In a few minutes, both of them were seated by Govind's desk as they went through the presentation that Govind had prepared.

"What do you think, Dhia?" asked Govind.

"This is really impressive, Govind. Your proposal resonates strongly with me. Especially with getting the next level of leaders to work on the project, the idea of a team coach, and your strong sponsorship. The timelines seem a real challenge but you've listed the priorities well and this is exactly what the Council wants. Just a question, have you got anyone in mind for the team coach?" asked Dhia.

"Yes, I do. Have you heard of Pietr, the peacock who is the executive and team coach? He did some great work at ACE Inc., MIB, and some of the big banks," said Govind.

"Pietr? Yes, I know him personally. He was my mentor when I was at college. I can vouch for his character and results," said Dhia. "He's actually one of the best in the field of team coaching—I cannot think of anyone better—and I was going to recommend him to you anyway."

"That's really great! I've set up a meeting with Pietr for later this week. Would you like to join us? Since you know him personally, perhaps there is a chance that he would be agreeable to work with us?"

"I'd be glad to. Let me know the exact date and time and I'll free up my schedule for you. By the way," Dhia continued, "I'm just wondering, since we only have you on the agenda at the Council Meeting tomorrow, what plans you have in mind for when you become our CEO."

"Huh? What do you mean?" asked Govind, rather surprised at what Dhia had said.

"Your plans when you take over as CEO, Govind. Tomorrow could be a good time to pick the brains of the Council, don't you think? You are a planner and even though it's a few months down the road before you take over the helm at WILD, I know you would have thought through this quite carefully," said Dhia.

"Actually, no. I've not given it any thought," mumbled Govind. Realising that Dhia would want him to say more, Govind continued, "It's all a bit strange, isn't it, Dhia? Lang, the proposed change in leadership—all this feels like a dream to me. Is it really happening? I know, I know. Osman himself told me. But I was hoping that it's not true. I was hoping that everything will be normal at the Council Meeting tomorrow—Liu will be in charge, Lang next in line, and so forth. I'm totally 'chill' for Lang to be the next CEO as this is how it has always been. I mean, for the lions to be in charge of WILD. I'm not sure I'm ready for any change … and for me to be CEO. This doesn't happen at the WILD Company, not even in my wildest dreams would I ever imagine that I could become CEO of WILD. Do you know what I'm saying, Dhia? Why the Council chose me, I haven't a clue …" Govind looked incredibly lost and insecure.

Dhia fluttered in front of Govind, putting on as fierce a face as she could muster, given that she's the kindest soul ever in the whole WILD organisation. "Govind, get real. The decision has been made. There is no turning back. Not even Liu can change the decision. Even if you die tomorrow," Dhia gave a big shudder at this thought, "even if you die tomorrow, Govind, Lang will still not be CEO. Some other animal will be found to take on the leadership role. Maybe a Council member in the interim, who knows? But it will not be Lang. At this moment, Lang is no longer on the list of potential CEOs. So get this out of your head. You are the assigned leader, and you have to start thinking and acting like one. From this moment on. Else you will not be ready to face the Council tomorrow. Do you hear me? Are you aware of what's happening? Do you understand what I'm saying?"

Tired out after that long lecture, which was probably one of the longest speeches ever spoken by Dhia in mid-air and in such a strong tone, Dhia flew to the table to catch her breath.

As Govind let her words sink in, Dhia went on. "One final point, Govind. What do you need to do to make the Council agree to your proposal? Let me venture a guess—a solution that focuses only on the situation or one that will also bring a new and refreshing style of leadership that the whole company can benefit from?"

"But … but … what … you mean …?" Govind started stuttering. Then all of a sudden, he realised the enormity of the tasks ahead of him "So, what you're saying, Dhia, is that if I can pull off a solution that strengthens their decision of me as CEO, that they had indeed made the right decision, I would get the approval I need?"

"Well done, my friend!" Dhia cooed happily. "You've got it! And I am so happy to be your A&C Business Partner! So, shall we go through your presentation and make the necessary edits?"

06
COUNCIL MEETING

Govind was indeed the only agenda item listed for the Council Meeting that day. "So, Dhia was right. I am the CEO-designate," thought Govind, when he saw the agenda projected on the screen in the Council Room. Feeling rather nervous yet resolute in his belief that things will work out well, he started his presentation. In a clear, calm voice, he started speaking.

All those present in the room were listening attentively to Govind's words, taking notes and not interrupting him until he asked, "Any questions?"

The Council Members started asking questions—and they were flowing fast in all directions.

"What do you mean, a 360—what is that? Some sort of mathematical formula?" Eisha asked in bewilderment.

"What's wrong with the way this company is working? Many companies I know work in the same way, even my own company. Why do you have to change this?" another Council member chipped in.

"Why do we need to develop SET further? They are all senior leaders. At that level, they should be leading and developing others, not being developed themselves!" scoffed an elderly member.

Another voice was heard asking, "What is a coach? What is coaching?"

And the voices kept coming in fast and furious.

"What is a team coach? What game are we playing here? I don't follow what you're saying, Govind!"

"This seems to be a big waste of time to me!"

"This is all gibberish to me. Just get them to do the tasks they have to do and things will work out eventually!"

"I honestly do not believe Lang would even agree to this. He needs a psychiatrist, not a coach!" Eisha drawled, looking directly at Liu as she said this.

"How much is this whole thing going to cost? Do we even have the budget for this?"

Govind waited patiently until everyone had their turn and then he spoke.

"Thank you for your questions. I will now respond to all of them. Firstly, the budget. As I had mentioned earlier, I will not be requesting for any extra budget. Year in, year out, we set aside an amount of money for Animal and Culture to spend on animal development activities. Year in, year out, this money is not spent. As we are now only mid-way into the financial year, with not a single penny touched, I propose we use this to pay for the coaching activities that I would like to have in place."

Govind then looked around the room, and as he spoke, he paused a few seconds to look each one in the eye. "Yes, we have been the same as the other organisations. That was in the past. But now we are in a mess. Animals are leaving for NEON and DUMA. Who knows where else they are going to. And we can't replace them quickly enough. We also have a culture of some bad behaviours, in particular, how we protect our own turfs, complaining and blaming others. There is a lack of responsibility and ownership. We are shouting, growling, throwing tantrums, breaking furniture, taunting and hurting each other with verbal abuse, and the list goes on. We are all guilty of these bad behaviours. I, too, am guilty—ready to point a paw at others, not helping when I could have done so.

"If I were to just lead the team that is working to resolve this situation, I will be comfortable to just have a coach for this team. But if I am, and this is what I see on the slide, the CEO-designate of WILD, I want to be able to work with a team that I will inherit in a few months' time. Animals who are my peers, one of them who is my best buddy, but all who will report to me when the time comes. Not only do I have to lead the SET, but I have to also lead the whole company, to bring this company back on its feet again." Govind let this sink in before continuing.

"So, who is this coach I am planning to work with? First of all, this is someone who can help us understand ourselves better, to be more aware of the impact we have on others, why we behave the way we do. This will be done through some tools and analyses, what I have referred to as the 360.

"Secondly, this coach will help us develop our strengths and, in the process, recognise our weaknesses.

"Thirdly, we will learn to work together as a team—to collaborate with each other, to appreciate each other's diverse views, to show that we can all work together with trust and respect, where silos are broken and problems are solved.

"I want the leaders to lead by example, to role model good behaviours. I want them to speak a language of respect and trust. We see bad conduct across teams because the leaders themselves are behaving badly. They are encouraging the cascade of these bad behaviours. I want these changed.

"I want employees to feel they are being listened to, teams to consult broadly, and individuals to build on each other's ideas to deliver successful business outcomes, without fear of being told off or excluded just because they are too junior or lack experience. If this is to happen, then the change in behaviours has to come from the very top. Like it or not, this means the Senior Executive Team—we have to walk the talk.

"This may sound rather far-fetched to some of you, but I believe that's what you are thinking right now. I've heard good things about Pietr, the coach I intend to hire to work with us. He's done great work in ACE Inc., MIB, and some of the big banks. If I'm not mistaken, Osman, Pietr was hired by your organisation too, wasn't he?"

Before Osman could respond in the affirmative, Eisha jumped, causing the whole building to shake. "What? You mean you hired a coach for your team at JSB Inc.? Osman? Why haven't you mentioned this before?"

It was now Osman's turn to drawl. "Well, if I did, none of you would have heard Govind's discourse. And you would not appreciate the seriousness of the situation. You are now hearing this straight from the gorilla's mouth— plain and simple."

"Well, then, if the Chair of the WILD Council has a coach for his own organisation, who are we to say 'nay' to this now, especially since there is no need for additional money out of our coffers," Eisha reasoned.

The Council of Leaders

Osman   **Eisha**

"Yeah, but have you forgotten Lang? Liu? You've been silent all this while. How would Lang react to this? He's not going to buy all this, surely?" asked another Council member, anticipating Liu to come out strongly against Govind's proposal.

Liu stood up, squared his shoulders, and in a low tone said, "Lang will abide by the decision of the Council. It no longer matters what his view is. The company reputation is at stake and I would expect that he participates fully in turning the company around, like the rest of the SET. Govind, you have my word on this."

Osman took the silence as the opportunity to get a full mandate from the Council, "So, all in favour of Govind's proposal say 'Aye'".

"AYE!!"

07
LANG:
THE THREE QUESTIONS

Seated in Dhia's office, Lang was impatiently waiting to meet his assigned coach. Dhia had advised him of the importance of getting to know each other, to be able to build an atmosphere of mutual trust, respect, and honesty, where a safe space is created so Lang could be open and vulnerable, sharing his innermost thoughts and feelings without fear of being judged. Most important was that both Lang and his coach had to have the right chemistry together, and believe that they both could create and build a sound coaching relationship for Lang to learn and grow.

Lang was beside himself with excitement. "I'm getting a coach. Wow! I'm getting a coach. I'm going to learn more about myself and I know that I will be absolutely superb." Immediately upon thinking this, Lang started to feel apprehensive. "What does it mean to be vulnerable? Why do I have to expose my feelings? Why do I need a coach? Why can't they leave me alone? Why can't I be who I want to be? What if I don't meet expectations? What if I fail? Why did Father set me up for this?"

Lang could think no further as the door opened and Gao entered Dhia's office. One look at her and Lang was completely astounded. His thoughts raced. "What?! A female giraffe?" He looked at Dhia, who was welcoming her with delight and thought: "What's this? Is that giraffe giving Dhia a hug? Why on earth would they be hugging each other? What is going on?"

Lang was in a daze. And it felt surreal as Dhia introduced them both, happily sharing Gao's achievements. She then flew out of the room, leaving them both facing each other.

Lang's thoughts were interrupted by a deep yet friendly voice. "Would it be good if we sat down, or would you prefer to stand?" asked Gao politely.

Not realising that he was actually standing stiffly on all his four legs, Lang got a hold of himself and said, "Hrmmpphh, okay. Let's sit down then." And under his breath, he muttered, "Else my neck will be completely stiff in five minutes!"

Once they were both seated, Gao started, "Perhaps I ought to share a bit about myself first, so you get to know me better. At the same time, would you like to tell me something about yourself? If you don't mind, I would like to take some notes, which I'd be happy to share with you later."

One look at her kind face and everything started to come out. Lang wasn't quite sure how this happened but he started talking about his childhood years, the pranks he played, the punishments he got, the grooming to be the next CEO, the current situation, etc. He just didn't give her time to talk or ask questions. He just talked and talked and talked … and all she did was nod and listen. Lang sensed she was listening to him because she looked directly at him, wrinkling her brows at times, tilting her head as she took notes—although she didn't seem to be taking too many notes. "And she's got the kindest face ever," Lang thought. When he paused for breath, Gao took the opportunity to summarise what she had heard.

Lang thought: "Wow! When she replayed what she heard me say, I felt like crying. She knew me, she got me, she understood me …. Strange, I've not cried since I was a cub. But wow! She evoked some really strong emotions in me."

"Hang on a minute," thought Lang as his mind switched tracks, "is this what a coach does?" Lang didn't quite understand the emotions that were going through him. He felt uncomfortable at times as she was asking some really deep and profound questions that he'd never considered before and they touched a raw nerve in him. At the same time, he felt like, at last, there was someone who seemed to completely understand him. "Why am I feeling so light and yet so heavy at the same time?" he wondered.

Their discussion continued way past the designated hour. Dhia flew in to check on them and, with a sigh of relief, said, "Well, without much sound for me to hear through the doors, I couldn't guess if you had killed her, Lang, or that your conversations were so fruitful that time just stood still for you both. But I can see that you have great chemistry together, even though you are both so different." Dhia smiled when Lang nodded and tilted his head a little. Dhia blinked as she thought, "If I'm not mistaken, he just gave me a wink." She smiled to herself. "Ah well, wonders will never cease to happen."

Turning to the two of them, Dhia said, "So, I will leave you both to plan your sessions and the outcomes that you would like to achieve, Lang. All that's left for me to say is … take care and all the very best with your coaching sessions!"

LANG'S CHALLENGE

Feeling pleased with how the coaching session went with Gao, Lang strode off quickly to a scheduled meeting with his team. That afternoon, the meeting agenda included a discussion with Zack, the Sales VP, for a rundown on the figures so that they could review their strategy for the rest of the year. "I'd expect Zack to be there, that good-for-nothing zebra. He's always skiving off and not giving his butt-worth to the organisation. I wonder who his sponsor is in the company? He's been able to cover his tracks all this time, even though we all know how lazy and incompetent he is." Lang's thoughts ran sour and he wasn't feeling so good now, thinking about how Zack was the weakest link in the organisation and what everyone had to do, including putting in extra time to help out.

Looking around the meeting room as he entered, and in a rather loud voice, Lang said, "So, there we have it again, Zack's not here. Aren't we supposed to have him on the agenda this afternoon?"

Ting, Lang's competent right-hand, spoke, "Zack sends his apologies and Aang is here to represent Sales."

Lang growled, "What is the use of having a replacement for this meeting? Who is Aang? I've never met or seen him before. How can he give us the necessary sales figures? How can we work on the plan? I bet Zack is skiving off again. He doesn't dare to face up to the fact that his team is a mess and can't even execute the Sales plan!"

"You!" thundered Lang, pointing at Aang who was looking rather distressed and uncomfortable. "Give me the numbers now!"

As Aang spoke, Lang started to question every aspect of his presentation. His queries came quick and fast. "Why are you proposing such a long sales cycle? Didn't we agree with Zack to have this shortened? What do you mean this wasn't the agreed strategy?"

Aang tried to stammer out his replies but Lang cut him short. "Well, your sales teams have never had effective follow-up calls. All the customers are complaining to me. What are you doing about that? Where are your plans on this? I want to see them NOW." Before Aang could even move a muscle, Lang changed the topic. "Why haven't you involved my team when you visit our key customers. I told Zack months ago that we must work together. Why didn't you do so? Look at what this has done to our numbers!"

Lang then blustered, "You're all just hopeless. Completely wasting my time here. Why we even have you in our team, I have no idea."

The meeting went downhill from there. Lang was not satisfied with every response that Aang gave. Even if the numbers looked good and the analysis was a balanced one, Lang did not care. He was clearly in a mood to destroy everything that Aang said and proposed. The atmosphere in the meeting room was exceptionally toxic. Every animal's head was hanging down from their necks. No one dared to make a sound. No animal dared to speak.

When he saw every animal looking down, looking so cowardly, Lang got into an even worse temper. In anger and frustration, he got up to leave. Before stepping out of the room, he turned around and said, "This is the worst meeting ever. None of you are prepared. The figures are so weak—how can I expect you bunch to deliver success for WILD? All of you do not deserve a job at WILD!" And with that parting shot, he left the meeting.

FEEDBACK FOR LANG

Ting managed to find Lang before he left for home. "Err … Lang, I wonder if you've got some time right now? Could you spare me a few minutes please?

"This may not come out so well but I feel that I really have to talk with you." Taking a deep breath, Ting let it out. "I felt really uncomfortable at the meeting just now."

"You don't say," answered Lang. "I was really uncomfortable too. Zola came to talk to me about that too and we both agreed that Aang was spouting nonsense. What was he trying to say? Why did he come to the meeting when he's not prepared to speak? And when he does speak, he talks gibberish. How can we have a meeting like this? The head of function doesn't show up and his representative can't give us the information we need. It's so important to have Sales give a good view of where we are at as we need to recover from the situation. But Aang didn't do anything of that sort. He's absolutely pathetic!"

"I have a different view from you, Lang," Ting said softly and hesitantly.

"What? What did you say?" Lang asked, a bit startled with what Ting was saying. This was the first time she was speaking up to him and that piqued his curiosity.

Gaining confidence that Lang would not shout at her, Ting continued. "As far as I can see, Aang gave some good analyses and recommendations, but you were not listening. You were busy interrupting him, challenging him, and asking him to speak up. He was indeed speaking up but you did not listen to him at all. And I felt that you were attacking him a lot."

"I was definitely listening to him. He wasn't making any sense! He is so spineless and incompetent. Zola totally agreed with me on this. You have to agree with me too. Why is it that you don't see this?" asked Lang.

"Perhaps we do have our differences on what we heard Aang say. But I wanted to speak on something else—the atmosphere in the room … and the discomfort I felt. Not only me, but the others too," Ting slowly and gently spoke. "It was unpleasant to see. Some of the animals were smirking when you shouted at Aang. Others looked like they were getting ready to run out of the room. Aang himself looked like he was going to cry. I really felt bad for him."

"I wasn't shouting at Aang," insisted Lang. "I was just telling him my views and I do have the right to do so. But I feel justified considering he was talking nonsense," declared Lang defensively.

Patiently, Ting tried another way to get through to Lang. "I don't mean any disrespect, Lang, but you *were* shouting and you were showing your annoyance at Aang, in front of every animal in the room. I have to say that I felt really bad, not only for Aang, but for everyone at the meeting, including myself. I didn't like it at all, especially when I saw the reaction of the others.

"And if you felt that Aang was talking nonsense, I believe some clarification is needed from you, instead of just telling him that it's best for him to leave. After all, we need Sales to be present at our meetings to help us with our marketing strategy. Aang's the right animal to do this as he's been doing all of Zack's work whilst Zack's off to wherever he goes to. We've essentially wasted two full hours and we're no better than where we were earlier today. What will we do now? We do need to involve the Sales team, and we do need their input so we can present to the SET by the end of THIS week."

"Let me work on that. Now you go on home. We will get all this settled tomorrow," Lang said.

As he got ready to leave the office, Lang realised that Ting had been right about the meeting. They had achieved nothing in the two hours! And if he was really being honest with himself, all the time was wasted on him venting his frustration and anger on Aang. He should have gone to Zack and hauled him into the meeting room instead of going off and attacking Aang. "Was I really attacking him?" thought Lang. "That was what Ting said."

"Oh dear, I did put my foot in my mouth. What's wrong with me?" thought Lang. "Why was I so hurtful to that antelope? He looked so pitiful that it makes me sick just thinking about him now."

Suddenly a thought stuck Lang. "Am I like that to all the other animals in the company too? Am I a bully?" Immediately he erased that thought from his mind. "NO WAY! I'm not like that at all."

REALISATIONS

Back in his office, Lang was preparing for his session with Gao. Time had flown by very fast and it was exactly a month since he first met Gao. A lot had happened since that day when his emotions fluctuated like a yo-yo—one moment he was excited and feeling really good about himself, the next moment he was angry, foul-tempered, and frustrated. He had managed to get the numbers from Zack—and it was indeed Aang who had done all the work—and with some effective planning and discussions, things are looking better at the WILD Company now compared to a month earlier.

So the conversation with Gao started with Lang reminiscing about the meeting on that eventful day. Lang was talking and sharing his side of the story.

"When nobody spoke up, I got so angry and mad to the point I could feel my blood boiling. They all have ears, a brain, and a mouth, so why can't they speak up? I expected an intelligent and capable analysis of the situation but not one single word came out from anyone. They were just not good enough!"

"If I understand you correctly, this happened a month ago? You seem really angry even when you are talking about that event now. I wonder what's really causing this anger inside you?" Gao asked.

"It's their incompetence! It's their inability to respond to my questions. Their answers are so weak, so lame. It's like they have just graduated from school, like a bunch of interns. I just cannot imagine that Aang is Zack's second-in-command. He has no capability whatsoever. How can he be qualified to represent Zack at our meeting? He's just a junior in the organisation."

"What did Aang do to get you so angry?" asked Gao.

Ignoring Gao's question, Lang went on. "You know what? All these years, these animals really got me on edge, irritated me. Those who keep silent and just stared wide-eyed, like that antelope, are the worst. They get stunned and look so stupid! It's just a waste of my time to even try to work with them. Why did we hire them in the first place? What was my Father thinking when he hired them! That Dhia is really incapable. And to think she's our VP of Animal and Culture. I expect her to hire only the best. And Zack … what a …"

Seeing that Lang was getting all excited and starting to blame every single animal for their incompetence, Gao stepped in and said, "I'm really sorry to interrupt you mid-sentence here, Lang, but I'm a little lost with what you're saying. So, if you could allow me to summarise what I'm hearing. What I hear from you was that at this particular meeting, a month ago, you got angry with all those animals because they were not competent? And those animals comprise your team members as well as Aang from Sales?"

Lang nodded. "Yes, and ..."

Gao interrupted again. "So, you have an opinion of every animal in that meeting room. And your view of each of them was that they were stupid, not good enough, a bunch of interns?"

Again, Lang nodded his head. Gao then looked directly into his eyes and asked, "I'm just wondering, if you think so negatively of each of them and their capabilities, what do you think their individual views of you would be like?"

Startled by how Gao changed the direction of the conversation, Lang could only ask, "What do you mean?"

Gao replied, "Well, every animal is free to make an assessment of others, or make a judgement of others—what you think of, have a view of, or even how you judge others, in the same way others would also form their own opinion of you. I was curious what they were thinking of you at that meeting a month ago? And right now, a month later? More specifically, what would Aang be thinking of you?"

"Ohhh ..." Lang finally understood and this reminded him of what Ting told him that day after the meeting. "I never thought of that. And this was exactly what Ting told me as well.

"That was the first time anyone had ever spoken to me like that. Having had time to reflect since, perhaps Ting was right ... well, partially, not fully. But she was indeed very brave to speak up like that to me. I did not like the way she spoke to me. It's complete disrespect. But she was calm when she spoke. I can still remember what she said. For her to say that I attacked Aang, that little antelope. I definitely did not! But what if she's right? What if I did attack that antelope—not physically but through my words? Am I really that mean?"

As much as he tried to ignore Ting's accusation of him, Lang failed to forget as it kept coming back to him at different times of the day, every day, ever since that event a month ago.

"Tell me more," prodded Gao, tipping her long neck to one side.

"I thought it was all rubbish when Ting and I had that conversation. But what you asked just now was quite powerful—'what would the others think of me'. I've never considered that before. Now it's made me think. Hmm … I don't really want to know the answer because …" Lang hesitated.

"Because …?" Gao asked patiently.

"Because it could open a big can of worms. My goodness! Just reflecting on those many times when I got really angry. Everyone must be quite terrified of me. Some of them actually cower when I pass by them in the office hallways. I don't think I want to know …" said Lang, shaking his head and looking rather dejected.

"Hmm … you are participating in the 360 exercise like everyone else, aren't you?" Gao asked. "The one Govind asked all the SET and the Task Force Team to do?"

"Oh yeah … THAT one …" said Lang. "I am told that I need to do that but …"

"I'm happy to work through that with you if you'd like …" Gao ventured. "But before that let me share with you a story. It's called the Three Questions, and it was written by Leo Tolstoy, a Russian author …" When Gao ended her story, Lang was so affected by what he had heard that he immediately took out his notepad and wrote these sentences to remind himself:

- When is the most important time? **Now**
- Who is the most important animal? **The one you are with**
- What do you do? **YOU CARE**

The coaching session then continued with discussions on whom Lang would request feedback from. With some trepidation, he sent requests to Govind, some of his peers, direct reports and … to Aang as well, for their feedback.

Lang realised that he did not like being so angry anymore. His brain kept playing a scene during that fateful meeting a month ago where all the animals seemed to be frozen with fear, followed by another scene where all of them looked so forlorn with their heads hanging down. He now knew that it was his behaviour that caused them to react in that manner.

He didn't like what he saw. If he wanted to have a different outcome, he had to do something about it. He had to change.

EVERY INTERACTION COUNTS

The time came for the two-day cross-functional team meeting. The session started as planned. Govind welcomed all the animals as they walked into the Council Room. Every function was represented. There was an air of nervous anticipation as all the animals realised the significance of this meeting and their role in it.

Besides Govind, there were six representatives from the different functions. While Govind was the VP of Operations, he was also the CEO-designate and team lead. To ensure that the Operations team was fairly and equitably represented, he nominated his trusted deputy, Olive the orangutan, to represent the Operations function and provide her valued opinions on that front. As the VP of Marketing, Lang had asked Ting the tiger to represent their function. As usual, Zack was skiving; so who better to represent Sales than Aang the antelope, who did all his work anyway and knew the function better than anyone else. The remaining three were Dhia the dove, VP of A&C; Bao the brown bear who was VP of Finance; and lastly, the company's General Counsel, Rahman the rhinoceros.

Dhia, Bao, and Rahman represented their own functions as they had smaller teams, and they wanted to be personally involved. Prior to this day,

Ting, Olive, and Aang were briefed by their respective bosses about this cross-functional team meeting, including why they were selected, and the expected outcomes to be delivered by this team. This was the first time in the WILD Company where staff from different functions would be brought together to form a team to work on a corporate project that required strict confidentiality, collaboration, and interaction across functions.

Liu attended at the start of the meeting. As did Osman as Chair of the Council.

After some introduction from Liu, Osman flew to his perch at the front of the room. He spoke clearly and succinctly, "You have all been carefully selected to be a member of this very important project. You are amongst our brightest, most capable leaders in the WILD Company. You have achieved many successes in your roles …" Osman paused, and looked at every animal in turn. "We now want you to work together, to deliver success for WILD. And I mean it—you all need to work TOGETHER. This is probably new for you as you have never truly collaborated before. But the WILD Company needs a change—a change in the way we work, communicate, engage with each other, and do business with our customers and suppliers.

"The timelines are short—just one month. We have high expectations that you will deliver amazing results. The Council expects regular progress updates from this team. We will interact with you frequently to give you our support, to help you untangle challenges that you may encounter along the way. Every interaction the Council has with you will count towards achieving the success we desire. This is an extremely critical project that you are working on. Liu and I will take our leave now. Remember, every single interaction you have with your colleagues that is positive, collaborative, result-focused will count towards achieving success for WILD. Over to you now, Govind."

And with that, Osman flew out of the room with Liu following after him.

Govind shared the agenda for the two-day meeting. He kicked off the session by sharing the project goals and expectations, including the one-month timeline to deliver on some key targets.

Next, there was the general round of introductions of the individuals in the room. Sitting quietly in the corner of the room was a peacock. He was noticed by every animal but ignored by all, until Govind called out to him. "Pietr, please come to the front of the room," said Govind. "Pietr will be our team coach for this two-day team meeting."

"Just imagine some of the great sports coaches in our country. Pietr's role is similar to those coaches—to build this team, to facilitate the discussions that we will be having, to bring out the best in each of us, to help us learn how to work together, to support us as we work on our assigned tasks and the challenges we may face. And Pietr will be with us for the whole duration of this critical project."

When it came to Pietr's turn to speak, he first requested permission to do a video recording of the day as he expected there would be learnings to be obtained. With a nod from Govind, Pietr started recording.

With every animal in full attention, carefully keeping a safe distance from each other and aware that the video was capturing their every move, they listened attentively to Pietr's words. And what Pietr said confused some of them—he elaborated on the expectations of each team member, requesting that they reflect on five statements, which he flashed up on the screen.

> - Appreciate the need to put the team priorities ahead of your own personal task priorities
> - Understand and value the contribution that each member will make to the team
> - Learn how to effectively support each other
> - Learn to have open dialogue, and to share your concerns or fears
> - Learn to build trust and respect for each other

The animals were then divided into two groups to discuss their understanding of the concepts that Pietr had just shared. They were asked to build on and rephrase these statements to something they would own, and to bring back their final version to share with the whole group. They had thirty minutes to complete this first task. These revised statements would then be consolidated and used as guiding principles for the team to follow whilst working on their project.

What started off as a seemingly simple request from Pietr turned out to be one of the most peculiar situations that arose.

RUCKUS!

"What do you mean trust and respect?""

"How can I establish trust and respect with Animal and Culture? You're always poking your beak into everything we do!"

"I have so many other priorities. Why do I need to prioritise this project?"

"Why am I in this team?"

"I don't like to work with Finance—you are all mean to Marketing!"

"Support the Sales team? Sales can't even support the whole business!"

"What a sorry mess you are all in."

"What value can Legal provide? All you do is say NO to everything we suggest and that we'll all end up in jail."

And this went on for a good fifteen minutes. In both groups, the animals—and there were only seven—were shouting, growling, roaring, and screaming at each other, over each other. Voices were raised. Faces were getting redder with the energies of asserting their views, being defensive, protecting their turf. The volumes kept increasing as each animal tried to get himself or herself heard above the noise.

Dhia started flying back and forth between the two groups, trying to pacify everyone, not realising that in the pandemonium, some of her feathers had got caught in Aang's antlers whilst Aang was shaking his head in fear and anguish.

Govind looked at Pietr, wondering when he would put an end to this chaos. Calmly, Pietr flew to the table, stretched out his neck and screamed loudly, "Aaaaaaaahhhhhhhh!" The sound he emitted was so shrill that every animal recoiled in shock and tried hard to cover their ears.

Silence.

The room was so quiet that you could hear a pin drop. Immediately, every animal stopped what he or she was doing or saying and looked at each other in shock.

"Wow, that was like a fish market. Well, at least that's what happens on market day, doesn't it?" said Pietr with a smile, fluttering his feathers slightly.

"Right, now that I've got your attention, let me say a few words. I can see that you've all had a chance to air your views. Very strongly. And with lots of energy. The impact on each of you was different. Some of you started talking even louder and faster. Some of you attacked your colleagues. Some of you ran away and hid. But I don't believe any group managed to accomplish the task I requested of you, correct?" said Pietr. All the animals shook their heads at this remark. "So, shall we replay the scene that just happened?" Pietr suggested. "I'm really glad I asked to record the session from the beginning of this day."

Pietr then proceeded to replay the video he had taken, and in slow motion. He asked every animal to observe his or her own behaviours as they watched the replay. "Don't focus on the topics that you were supposed to discuss. Just carefully watch your own reactions and behaviours."

"Oohh … I was talking all the time," said Olive.

"You were talking? You were screeching and screaming your head off and not letting anyone get a word in!" chimed Ting.

"I looked so angry! Is that how I look when I'm angry?" Rahman ventured.

"I was flying back and forth between the two groups trying to compare notes but ended up losing a whole chunk of my feathers!" said Dhia miserably.

"The three of us ended up fighting each other … and it was all your fault!!" Bao looked accusingly at Rahman and Govind.

Just then, Govind noticed that Aang was not with them. "Aang?" he called out. "Aang, where are you? Errr … why are you hiding under the table, Aang?"

Every animal looked under the table too. Aang was crouched on the ground, looking unhappy and miserable. "Maybe he's crying," thought Dhia. Pietr crawled under the table to talk with Aang. Whatever it was that Pietr said, Aang started to hesitantly crawl out from under the table whilst shaking his head from side to side.

"Aang …" Dhia started.

"Hang on, Dhia," Pietr said calmly. "Let's give Aang some space."

All the animals stepped back, looking at Aang as he slowly took his seat. "I don't know what came over me. I was so looking forward to this meeting. I really thought this would be different from all the other meetings we've had. But when the shouting and growling started, I got really scared … and disappointed. I should have been more prepared that this would happen. We're never going to be a team, ever! We're just behaving the same way as before. Whose idea was it to have this meeting?" Aang started sobbing.

"Thank you for sharing, Aang," said Govind softly. "Would it be good for us to have a short break now, Pietr? There's a lot to take in this morning. I know I need some breathing space."

"Yes, that's a good suggestion, Govind. Let's take a fifteen minute break. During this break, reflect on what you have learnt about yourself from what you saw on the video. See you back here after the break," said Pietr.

REFLECTIONS AND LEARNINGS

When the animals trooped back into the room after the break, Pietr requested they all sit down, stay calm for five minutes, simply observing their breathing, focusing their attention on their senses.

He then handed to each of them a stack of papers. "This is your 360 feedback report. It contains the scores you gave yourself as well as a summary of the scores from colleagues you had requested feedback from.

"We need to first understand ourselves—be aware of how we behave, how we act, who we are—before we can understand the impact we have on others—our colleagues, our friends, our loved ones. All of you experienced first-hand this morning and saw some rather negative behaviours and actions coming out of each of you.

"Now is a good time for you to dig a little deeper, to investigate, and be curious about yourself," Pietr emphasised.

The rest of the morning was spent understanding the 360 scores that they rated themselves and also the ratings from their colleagues, the dynamics and interrelationships of the scores, their strengths and weaknesses. It was a surprise to many—their personal assessments of themselves were very different from their colleagues' feedback. But all of them also agreed that the feedback was spot on, reinforced by what they saw on the video replay. It was indeed very painful to watch themselves in such light. But this was the evidence, proof that showed their true selves playing out. There was no way they could deny the existence of their bad behaviours.

With Pietr's support, all the animals in the room discovered more about themselves. They realised the impact of their behaviours on others, why sometimes they were not able to achieve the outcomes they wanted because of how they were showing themselves to others. They also appreciated the importance of building trust, being open and transparent, speaking their views in a way that everybody understood—what respect meant for each of them, giving air space to others and not just hogging the attention by talking non-stop.

Finally, Pietr said something so powerful that all the animals paid close attention. "There is a reason why you were chosen to be in this team. Acknowledging your strengths and accepting the need to develop further will help you achieve success in your personal and professional lives. At the same time, each and every one of you can complement each other to make this project a mega success, ONLY IF you learn to collaborate with each other. And I'm here to show you exactly what this will look like, if you will let me …"

Nodding their heads with understanding and agreement, the animals in the room got down to working on the tasks assigned to them. Extroverts gave the introverts space to reflect before speaking and in doing so, the extroverts realised that when they had time to think, the views of the introverts were more insightful and resonated well with everyone. Every animal began to slowly understand what it meant to respect each other's expertise and capabilities, appreciating that there was a need to seek Legal's input, getting Finance's support to help with the pricing, and for Sales and Marketing to take the time to talk with each other.

One important realisation that they had during the two days of intensive team-building activities was that it was okay to be affected by someone else's behaviour, what they said, and how they said things. But it was not okay to continue to begrudge their colleagues and not seek clarification. It was the first time all of them understood the power of providing constructive feedback to each other in a respectful way so that it did not hurt any of them; instead, it made them even stronger.

At the end of the two days, there was some semblance of a team coming into shape. And the name they created for the team was even more telling of how far they had journeyed together: the Triple C Team, or in full, the Curious, Courageous, and Collaborative Team.

COUNCIL PRESENTATION

The Triple C Team continued to meet on a daily basis, for an hour each time. Every animal was assigned tasks to work on. Progress of the team was fast and furious.

It was time for their first weekly update to the Council. Excitement and nervousness was prevalent in the Council Room.

Every team member took turns presenting. The data shared by the younger members of the team—Aang, Olive, and Ting—was impressive. As Aang was presenting the results of his investigation, Osman suddenly threw in a question about the sales target for the next five years. Caught completely off-guard, Aang stammered and said the first thing that came to his head. Immediately he realised that the response he gave was incorrect. Unfortunately, it was too late to give the correct numbers as the presentation had moved on.

A short break was called after the presentation. Feeling rather despondent about his lack of alertness when Osman threw him the curveball, Aang stood alone feeling really upset with himself for not being better prepared. Suddenly, Osman flew over to him. "Aang, how are you doing? Your presentation just now—nicely done. By the way, your response to my question about the sales target. I don't think that was quite correct, was it? Perhaps there were a couple of zeros missing?" smiled Osman.

"Yes, sir. I apologise. It was my mistake. Yes, I was two zeros off with my response," said Aang.

"Ahh … good to know. I just wanted to make sure you knew your numbers. And well, I did give you a bit of a surprise, throwing you that curveball question. Well, run along now, the session will restart soon. I'm eager to hear about your proposals." And with that Osman flew back into the Council Room.

"Wow! Osman came to talk with me! Wow! I thought I was going to get roasted, but I didn't. Wow! What did he say about my presentation? I missed that …" Although pleasantly surprised and encouraged with what Osman had said to him, Aang felt a tad disappointed that he failed to clearly hear what Osman said about his presentation.

THE FIRST STEP

Encouraged by all the Council Members' receptiveness and support, the Triple C Team was in a buoyant mood. Govind organised a team dinner that evening … and every animal was talking, laughing, and enjoying the company of the other. They had been through a lot together this past week, discovering something about themselves that they never knew, and also of each other. They still had a long way to go as there was still a lot to get done, but some firm friendships were slowly forming, for sure.

The weeks quickly passed and soon the Triple C Team was preparing for their final report to the Council. Ting and Olive found that they had so much in common, being young, female, and hungry for success. They both lacked the self-confidence that they could one day become leaders, not daring to imagine that, just perhaps, they could lead their own functions and earn the title of Vice President. Never in their wildest dreams did they dare to dream that they could be the CEO of a company … and definitely not CEO of the WILD Company. Thus, they naturally gravitated to each other.

"You know, Olive, I would like to do this with my team too—how Pietr weaved his magic with us. I still remember that first day of the team meeting, we were just so 'wild'. It sure wasn't easy in the beginning," said Ting.

"Yeah, you're right, Ting. I am sure we hated each other's guts then. But look at us now! And what we've achieved in just one month! I wonder, can we really do this same thing across our teams? What do you think? Building our own teams, work cross-functionally in a collaborative manner?" Olive asked.

Aang was sauntering by when he overheard Olive's last sentence, "What did you just say, Olive? Working in a collaborative manner?"

Ting waved Aang over to the spot next to her. She had seen a side of Aang she never noticed before—his innovative ideas, creatively working out solutions for the team whilst taking every function into account, never leaving any animal out. He had indeed transformed—from the frightened antelope to a proud and magnificent one. The hidden talents of Aang were revealed before their eyes. They discovered his sharp focus on details whilst maintaining the bigger picture, and his ability to always motivate the team. And boy, could he talk! He was able to hold his audience as he made a pretty good sales pitch. It was clear to all why he was in the Sales team.

Olive was clearly in a reflective mood. "You know what I want? I want to be able to work like how we've worked on the project during the past month—but I want to do this all the time. I want to be in a place where I can smile and say 'hello' to everyone I meet in the corridor. I want my team to be able to go directly to seek advice from Rahman on legal issues and not get a grunt back from him. And for Bao, maybe sometimes, to say 'yes' if we make a robust and valid business case and therefore giving us more budget …

"I want a new culture in the WILD Company. That's it! I want to be able to change our company culture so that … hey!!" Olive was now getting excited and jumping up and down. "You know, like what we've done here—everyone to be curious, courageous, and collaborative with each other in the company! What do you think? Ting? Aang? Do you think this is achievable? How? What do we need to do?"

Aang was getting excited too. "Well, I know what I want! All our leaders to make time to talk with the staff. Did I share with you what Osman did?" Ting rolled her eyes. "Yes, a zillion times already …" Ignoring her, Aang said, "I want all leaders to behave the way Osman did. He definitely walks the talk. He makes every single interaction count, all the time, every time.

He doesn't differentiate. He is kind. He helps us learn, grow, and develop. He is truly a wise leader."

Ting scoffed, "Aang's gone gaga over Osman yet again. Well, what I want is for everyone to be brave enough to speak the truth. Give honest, truthful feedback in a respectful manner. Be able to receive feedback even though it may hurt them, for a while. To see beyond the hurt and appreciate the courage of the giver to share that feedback—especially if it is negative feedback—be it to someone more senior or junior than themselves. To me, this is freedom of speech, freedom of giving the gift of feedback to anyone we believe deserves our gift. Creating a new language for all of us to speak with each other!"

"Well, why don't you include all these in your proposal to the Council then?" a voice in the dark spoke. And slowly emerging from the dark was Govind.

"Huh? Govind? When … when did you sneak … err, we meant we didn't realise you heard us, Govind," Olive recovered herself, but not nearly in time.

Govind continued speaking. "As I was saying, why don't you include these ideas as part of your proposed solution to the Council? We've included all the technical resolutions and process improvements we can think of. Things are in place to happen. But we can't just change the organisational structure, the policies, and processes. The animals have to change too. They must want to change. We need to build a different culture. And we will need to create a new language to support this change. We have to get our staff excited, to look forward to a new way of working in our company." Govind paused, to assess if they were following him.

He continued, "The project took us one month to complete. We met daily. We worked through the night. We didn't work well together in the beginning, but we ended up working very well together. We can definitely proudly call ourselves a team now. We need to continue to build on the camaraderie, the collaboration, across the organisation. We can't let all this go to waste after this work is done. There is a danger that when we go back to our day jobs, everything could just fall apart."

Govind then said, "You three can be the ambassadors of change in our organisation. What would you like to see happen? What do you want from the Council to help you achieve your dreams of working in the WILD Company?" With that, he ambled off, leaving the three of them wide-eyed and open-mouthed, their hearts beating with excitement.

09
GOVIND: LIVING A LIFE OF AUTHENTICITY

BEING AN AUTHENTIC LEADER

Olive caught Govind just as he was leaving the office for the day. "Govind, may I speak with you? Just for a few minutes."

"Sure, Olive. What would you like to talk about?" enquired Govind.

"Govind, what did you mean when you said that the three of us are ambassadors of change? I don't quite follow what you asked of us earlier today," Olive asked.

"Oh, I just happened to be passing by. None of you heard or saw me so I thought I'd listen in. The three of you got really excited and passionate about those good things you were talking about. If I recall correctly, your conversation was about a culture change where we work towards making every interaction count, and being courageous to give and receive feedback. Did I hear you all correctly?" Govind asked.

Olive nodded vigorously, encouraging Govind to continue. "Well, my question to you, if I remember correctly, was what would you like to see happen in the WILD Company, that now would be a great opportunity for you to make this request to the Council, to seek their support for that." Govind said.

"Well, yeaahh. We discovered we enjoyed each other's company during the past month. We learnt a lot and realised that the earlier assumptions we had about each other were totally incorrect. We want to continue to work together even after this project is over. If we could work like this all the time, that would be superb!" Olive said enthusiastically.

"You seem really excited about this, Olive. What do you need to make this happen?" asked Govind.

"Well, there are a few things that come to mind. Firstly, I want all my direct reports to undergo what we went through—do a 360 to understand themselves, then learn how to work as a team. I want to do what Pietr did with our project team. So when I work with them, we speak the same language, and can work effectively together to achieve our targets. I know Ting and Aang also want the same thing with their teams. Imagine, when we work on future cross-functional projects, we can talk to each other and our teams can also talk to one another. The silos, fears, distrust would evaporate, and we can work collaboratively towards the same goals. No more double or even triple rework! Think about it—Sales and Marketing working together. Wouldn't that be amazing?

"Secondly, if we could see all SET members walk the talk, behaving in the same way. That would be completely awesome! You are all our role models, and if you can do that, everyone else would follow in your footsteps.

"Finally, it would be great if all employees could get some basic soft-skills training. Not just technical, on-the-job training but also training on how to work effectively together. I believe it would really help change how we behave towards one another. I truly believe that every animal wishes to succeed and be happy at work, as well as be able to make new friends across functions. Ting is so nice, and actually, so is Aang. I would never have imagined that Aang is so visionary and so smart if I wasn't part of this project team. I would totally have imagined the worst of him if not for being part of Triple C," said Olive.

Govind nodded. "You've made some good points Olive. Is there anything else? I'm happy for you to just think big, to reach for the sky …"

"May I say this? I'm not sure if it's going to cause any problem but …" Olive eyed Govind hesitantly. Seeing his encouraging demeanour, she decided to give it a go. "If we could have more effective decision making. We were so effective, the Triple C Team. We took ownership and responsibility; we did our homework. When it was time to make decisions, we did them fairly and quickly. We listened to each other, no interruptions, no talking over each other. Rahman and Bao respected our views and supported us.

They were constructive in sharing with us what would work and what would not. They were so different from what we know of them in the past! We even learnt more about each other and our relationships grew deeper and stronger. I want this to continue. I want every animal to experience what we did. There is no turning back. There, you asked me to reach for the skies! That's what I want to see happen!" Olive said emphatically.

"I hear you, Olive," said Govind, as an idea started to build in his mind. "Yeaahh, I can see that happening. I can see that you've got really good ideas. To implement them, we need a team. Perhaps you could start thinking a bit more and we meet tomorrow morning to discuss this further. If this is going to be an additional proposal to the Council, we need to act fast."

"Right! I will work on it immediately," Olive jumped happily up and down and ran off to look for Ting and Aang.

Govind felt really good. He believed he was indeed coaching Olive, or perhaps he was having a coaching conversation with Olive. And he was being truly authentic—true to himself and his purpose of helping Olive to grow. This was a great start. He felt happy and confident, knowing that he could help others to grow. Perhaps there were others in the company who had a similar passion too.

When the day of the final presentation to the Council arrived, there were no surprises. The Council had been keeping tabs on the progress of the Triple C Team so they knew what was going on. The message was clear: Take all proposals forward. Every aspect of the proposals, including creating a new culture in the organisation, was approved. "Just go and make it happen," said Osman. Osman's words kept resonating in their ears.

And so it came to be. One single act of courage to propose change in the WILD Company secured the support from the senior leaders in the organisation. And this was a change that would see fruition because it came not from the top but from the animals that mattered most to the organisation.

Thus, the deployment to change the culture across the WILD Company was approved by the Council. A task force, comprising Olive, Ting, Aang, and a few others, set about looking into how the change was to be rolled out. They came up with a list of actions—which were subsequently also approved by the Council—and had these printed on cards for the task force, SET, and the senior leaders to remind them of what they had to aim for.

- Every line manager will be trained to equip himself or herself with foundational coaching skills.
- Coaching champions will be identified across all functions and they will receive the necessary training e.g. individual coaching and team coaching. Coaching will be provided to as many as are genuinely interested to develop themselves further.
- A network of learning is to be created to support the coaching champions and line managers, to share best practices and learn from their successes and failures.
- A new language will be created and all staff are to be trained to use this new language for effective communication, to help them develop their curiosity, be courageous to give and receive feedback, and to collaborate with colleagues across functions.
- Key Performance Indicators will be defined to assess effectiveness of intervention.
- Executive coaching is to be extended to the second-in-command in each function and other high performers as identified by SET.

And so the journey had begun …

A journey of a thousand miles begins with a single step.
—Lao Zi, *Dao De Jing*

10
BRAND NEW WILD INC.

LANG'S CHAT WITH GOVIND

As the day of the town hall approached, Govind sought Lang out. He wanted to have a conversation with Lang prior to the announcement that he, Govind, would be the next CEO upon Liu's retirement. Govind did not have a chance to follow up on the conversation he and Lang had had when they were informed of the Council's decision many months ago. Now was the right time to do so, before they got caught up in the excitement surrounding the announcement.

"Hey, Lang, do you have a minute?" Govind caught sight of his friend as Lang was walking towards the entrance of the WILD building. "Govind," acknowledged Lang with a nod and a hint of a smile.

"It's been some time since we caught up, Lang. How are things at your end?" Govind asked. Lang stopped walking and looked at Govind, "Never been better, Govind. Say, shall we take a walk? I'll just drop some things off and we'll meet by the lake in ten minutes?" said Lang.

Govind nodded. "See you then, Lang."

In ten minutes, both Govind and Lang were at the lake, looking into the still waters and enjoying the peace and quiet of the early morning.

"Let's walk to our hideout," said Lang. "I've not been back there since THAT day."

As they were walking, memories of their past came flooding back and they started reminiscing about the times they had fun together, when they played tricks on their friends and families, and also the times when they were punished for the mischief they caused. As the hideout came into view, their laughter ceased and they paused. "Hmmm … it is pretty bad, isn't it?" said Lang. "Indeed! It's completely flattened. Like a bomb blast!" laughed Govind.

"I've changed, Govind," said Lang, turning to look directly at his old friend. "I'm no longer angry with Father, with Osman, or with you. I have come to realise that I, and I alone, chose the path of anger and destruction. At that time, I felt that I had the right to be, as I was the prince-in-waiting for the throne. I was angry at everything, blaming everyone for the mistakes that I made. I know now that I can choose a different path—one where I take full responsibility for the choices I make, own up to them, and move on. And now I feel so much better for this. You know what, I feel so much happier now than I've ever been."

Govind smiled. "I can see the transformation in you, Lang. You do look happier these days, more relaxed. There is an air of peace around you somehow. And your eyes—that mischievous glint is back. I can see it clearly now. But Lang, I too have changed," admitted Govind. "I used to think that there were many things I could not do, or I wasn't sure if I could ever do. But somehow, I realised that I am the one who is stopping myself from growing. I am my own worst enemy. And when I broke down this barrier, I see myself with so much potential. It is quite enlightening."

"You know, even though we never talked much during the past few months, I have been observing you from a distance. You are going to be great as our new CEO!" Lang smiled.

"You have? Hah! I've been watching you too, Lang. How you led your teams, how your laughter reverberates through our offices, how Ting speaks so well of you when we have our team meetings. I see you have grown so much in such a short time. I am so happy of the change you've become."

"Hey, let's not get too touchy-feely here. Say, let's rebuild this hideout. Let's start anew, shall we? If not for ourselves, then for our kids and their kids. We can do this all over again and make it even better. What do you think, Govind?" asked Lang.

"Just like old times, huh?" Govind said with a huge smile.

"Yeah … let's do the right thing, eh, Govind?" said Lang.

There was no need to say more. Enough had been said. Their friendship would last through the generations. And they knew what they each had to do.

TOWN HALL

And so, a new era began at WILD. Govind, the silverback gorilla, was announced as the new CEO of the WILD Company to all employees at the town hall meeting. This would have been unheard of just one year ago. But today, none of the animals seemed to care. Govind was known to all. In the past weeks, he had been holding regular dialogue sessions with the staff—in the canteen, at focus group sessions—to share the company's challenges in a way that the animals understood, and to also seek their views and potential support to implement those important changes that would have to be made across the organisation. Even though many animals were surprised when the announcement came, none of them were disappointed or upset. They welcomed the new CEO and looked forward to what was coming next.

There had been questions on why Lang was not CEO. During the town hall, Lang bravely stood up to talk about his role and to clarify any doubts the staff had. He had changed so much that many animals did not think it was truly Lang speaking. He looked the same—magnificent, proud, distinguished—but he spoke with a degree of calmness no animal recognised. A steady, yet wise, lion. The animals were curious—what made Lang change, how did he change, what did he do … they just had so many questions!

Although there were rumblings in the beginning, most of the staff were happy with the changes announced at the town hall. One of the animals unhappy with the change was Zack the zebra who had led the Sales function. Zack had left the organisation a few weeks ago. Never ever would he kowtow to a silverback gorilla. In his place—with a strong command from Osman, although there was little to disagree over—Aang was promoted to VP of Sales. A fitting successor. Aang had developed so effectively in the past months that he was the best candidate for the role.

This was indeed a different town hall from before. In part, there was a lot of dialogue during the Q&A session. The new CEO and members of his leadership team took turns to respond to the questions. At the same time, the Triple C Team also shared the stage. This was the first time the next level of leaders took to the stage to present the high-level overview of their project.

The message was clear for all to see. Govind wanted all staff to recognise the younger leaders, and to provide opportunities for them to be visible to everyone. There was another reason for doing so: to kick-start the vision of changing the culture at the WILD Company.

All the animals were asked to leave the main hall for the final item on the agenda.

KOKO KARA CAFE

Gathered at the wide, open field next to the main hall were Gao, Pietr, and Govind's coach, Lana.

The Coaches

The field was clearly marked with circles, and an equal number of animals were assigned to each circle. Every member of SET, Triple C, Gao, Pietr, and Lana stood in one of the circles to facilitate the discussions that were going to start. Osman, too, had volunteered to facilitate the session.

With a scream from Pietr, each leader started to work within their circle. Every twenty minutes, at the sound of Pietr's scream, the facilitators rotated. They moved to a new circle. The plan was to give all the animals a chance to engage with a leader in WILD, and a coach too. And what a wonderful hour all the animals had! The animals were delighted, even though in the beginning, some of them were cautious and apprehensive. For some, this was the first time they would come up close to a senior leader of the organisation. All of them were given a chance to air their views. Their voices were heard. They listened with interest to the plans that their leaders shared with them.

Ultimately, each employee had the chance to be in direct contact with at least one senior leader in WILD. And they had an opportunity to hear from a coach, to learn what coaching was all about, and the growth that could happen if they made the decision to change.

The hour flew by quickly. At the end of it, more animals came forward to volunteer their time to help turn the organisational culture around. New change champions were born.

In time, these champions of change worked together to create a new name for themselves—they called themselves leader-coaches. The simple criteria, included in their job descriptions, were: to have the passion to develop animals and the organisation; to have good coaching skills; and to be a role model to all in WILD. They also established the Koko Kara Café, modelled on the discussion activity they had during their town hall. Held once every quarter, it was to allow all employees, current and new, an opportunity to mingle with other staff and the leaders and coaches of WILD, hear another's views, and have their own opinions heard. This was how they kept the dialogue going and continually renewed the organisation's culture.

The
WILD Framework

A crisis can happen anytime, anywhere, at home, or at the workplace. It can impact anyone at the personal, work, company, or country level. There are many forms of crises—financial downturns, technological glitches, natural disasters … the list goes on. The Covid-19 pandemic impacted the whole world, with every human being affected in some way or another. Suffice to say every one of us would have experienced a few crises in our lifetime.

One can never be completely prepared when crisis or misfortune happens. The shock, the incredulity takes precedence. Depending on the severity, it may be days, weeks, or months before individuals can get over the shock that the crisis has happened or could have happened. The phase of finger-pointing or blaming others could take on a life of its own if not managed well, if leaders are not willing to take ownership and responsibility, like what happened at NEON.

With wisdom gained from experience, the period of getting over the initial shock could be shortened. Once this initial shock is over, an organisation that has built a strong foundation can be assured that its leaders will be able to steer their organisation out of the crisis. The accountability and ownership to lead with confidence, dedication, and trust will become second nature. It may take months or years to achieve this state of being. However, with a clear vision that is embraced by all, focus and persistence enhanced with strong and collective leadership, where all employees collaborate to create the right outcomes whilst living the company values, organisations are able to better manage any crisis. Or even at an elevated level, versus their competitors like what the WILD Company did in comparison to the NEON Company.

So, having invested in the development of their organisation over a period of time, the employees of WILD were able to cope with any crisis, as seen with the food poisoning scare in this fable.

But where and how did this all begin?

For the WILD Company, the journey started a few years back, when the senior leaders realised that things were not going well in the organisation. They made the brave decision to implement some sweeping changes which transformed the course of history for their organisation and how things were done there.

WHAT IS A COACHING CULTURE?

In 2003, E. Wayne Hart defined a coaching culture as: "An organisational setting in which not only formal coaching occurs, but also, most or a large segment of individuals in the organisation practise coaching behaviours as a means of relating to, influencing and supporting each other."

In his book, *Creating A Coaching Culture*, Professor Peter Hawkins stated that: "A coaching culture exists in an organisation when a coaching approach is a key aspect of how the leaders, managers, and staff engage and develop all their people and engage their stakeholders in ways that create increased individual, team, and organisational performance and shared value for all stakeholders."

Many books and articles have been written on the coaching culture and we share some of the references in the bibliography section of this book. David Clutterbuck's book, *Building and Sustaining a Coaching Culture*, has a summary of various authors' views on what a coaching culture looks like.

All of these definitions point to the premise that a coaching approach has to happen at all levels of the organisation—by line managers, human resource professionals, senior leaders, especially those in the C-suite. These leaders are role models that drive the company culture. They have to be seen using a coaching approach in every interaction, be it during meetings, during town hall sessions, when they meet with employees, and at external events. While the downstream effects will take time, employees will be motivated to follow suit when it begins at the very top of the hierarchy.

Apart from senior leadership paving the way, the following are some characteristics of an organisation where a coaching culture exists:

- Leaders have coaching conversations with employees and colleagues.
- Onboarding activities for new hires include modules on how to have coaching conversations.
- Leaders and line managers are trained on coaching methodology.
- Leaders and line managers have ready access to coaching tools.
- Employees have access to a pool of certified internal coaches.
- The organisation has a pool of certified external coaches who work with them at the individual, team, and organisational level.
- Employees at all levels take time to listen, to be open, curious, and supportive of each other.
- Shared leadership is the modus operandi and employees feel empowered to provide feedback on issues that matter.
- Teams are high-performing and value-adding.
- Cross-functional collaboration is the norm rather than the exception.
- Suppliers and vendors enjoy working with employees in the organisation.

THE WILD FRAMEWORK

There are numerous occasions throughout the fable where the WILD Framework to create a coaching culture at the workplace is demonstrated. We first present the Framework in its entirety followed by details, with examples of where and how these were presented in the fable.

In presenting the WILD Framework and our view of what characterises a coaching culture in an organisation, we believe that no barriers exist for anyone to work towards creating such a culture in their own organisation.

Figure 1 shows the four-step process to creating a coaching culture using the WILD Framework, an acronym that stands for **aWareness, Investigation, Language, Deployment.**

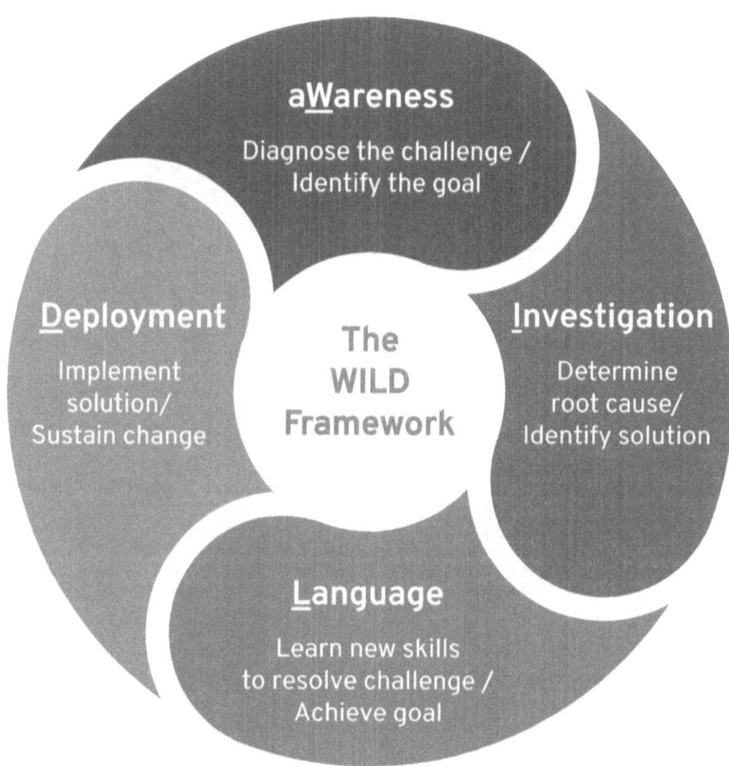

Figure 1: The four elements of the WILD Framework.

A<u>W</u>areness

"Awareness is the greatest agent for change."
—Eckhart Tolle

Through reflection, curiosity, and insight, it takes wisdom to become aware that things are not working out. It takes courage to share the anxiety or discomfort when things do not turn out the way we planned. It is often the bearer of bad news who risks putting his or her head on the chopping board. And to articulate this discomfort to a senior leader, or someone who is known for a bad temper in the organisation, can build some strong barriers within an individual to not even share his or her view and instead walk away in frustration or disappointment.

As you read through the chapters of the fable, were there moments when some of the characters' behaviours seemed to come to life for you? Perhaps you've experienced a Lang in your midst—angry, shouting, blaming everyone, banging tables, claiming ignorance and innocence ("It's not my fault!"), etc.?

If mistakes are made in the office setting, where does the blame land? How have you or your colleagues reacted to such bad behaviours at the workplace? Or is there a culture of strong ownership and responsibility?

In this fable, the characters became more aware, and understood themselves, their behaviours and actions better from the feedback they received. Here are some examples in the fable where the leaders became aware of the impact they had on others. Some of these were when feedback was offered in a safe space where trust and respect was a given and the conversation was calm, with emotions held at bay.

- Lang, when he received feedback from his father and Osman on his behaviour at the Council meeting.
- Ting, who bravely spoke with Lang after Lang walked off in anger when the meeting with Aang did not turn out the way he had wanted.
- The surprise the cross-functional team got when Pietr replayed the video showing their actions and behaviours as they worked on the expectations together.

Table 1 lists some questions that could help to evoke awareness, be it at the individual, team, or organisational level.

- Looking back at the past six months,
  - What was your proudest moment? Why?
  - What is one area that you would like to do better? Why?
- What are you good at and how have you demonstrated these skills in your daily work?
- What are your strengths and how have these strengths helped you achieve success?
- How are decisions made in your team?
- What are your customers or stakeholders saying about you, your team, or your organisation?

Table 1: Some questions to ponder during the aWareness stage.

But what happens if you have leaders who are not aware and think that everything is fine e.g. Lang at the time of his outburst? Can someone like Lang realise the impact of his behaviour on others, and also on himself? Will someone like Lang have the awareness that his inability to manage himself has caused him the CEO position in his organisation? Or what if you have leaders who know that things are not right but are not willing to admit it to others and the outside world, preferring to couch it in niceties e.g. Liu in his initial conversation with Govind? It is not so easy to say "be the first to speak up" because your job may be on the line.

Eckhart Tolle's quote sums up awareness nicely for an individual, team, or organisation. Coaching helps fast-forward this awareness through a thought-provoking inquiry process that a coach uses to help clients discover more about themselves. It is during this discovery journey that the decision to change happens.

The first step in the WILD Framework helps set the stage in giving guidance towards achieving awareness, through the wisdom of insight not only from others, but also through deep reflection within the individual.

In summary, it all begins with awareness. Being aware that things are not right. Diagnosing the issue and identifying some activities that can be done differently. Realising that some of our behaviours are not progressive and may have a negative impact on others and even ourselves. With awareness comes the decision to change and to improve, to identify and set goals. It is also the desire to do things differently that would have a more profound, positive, and lasting impact on everyone.

INVESTIGATION

When faced with a challenging situation, it is not uncommon to instantaneously lay blame on a difficult person, an angry customer, or the bureaucracy. But is this really the root cause of the problem? What has been our role in all of these? Could we also have played a part, albeit a smaller part, in causing the situation? The wisdom of Albert Einstein's words come into mind: What is the basis of the complaint or accusation that we make? Where is the evidence?

In the fable, despite being the difficult, angry colleague, Lang had a good friend in Govind. Even though others may not like working with Lang, Osman, Govind, and even Dhia spoke to Lang with kindness and care. What reflections do you have in this regard—who have you found difficult to work with only to find that others, perhaps even the colleagues you work well with, enjoy working with this overbearing, obnoxious colleague? Is this colleague the one that is difficult, or are you the one? How have you sought to investigate what lies behind the angry, difficult façade before making the judgement that he or she is indeed problematic to work with?

In order for a holistic investigation to take place, the concept of being open-minded and curious comes to the fore. Are our assumptions of that colleague being difficult accurate? What about the rigid behaviour of the management—what caused the leaders to behave in this way? Be open to question yourself on whether others also find this individual difficult, not accepting things as you see them but challenging yourself to gather the evidence first before jumping to a conclusion. Table 2 lists some questions that could be helpful at the investigation phase.

- What is the disparity between what you want to achieve and where you are now?
- What got in the way of you attaining your desired outcomes?
- From the 360 feedback that you obtained, what have you discovered about yourself?
- What feedback have your customers or stakeholders given to you?
- How comfortable are you with giving feedback to others?

Table 2. Some questions to ponder during the Investigation stage.

In the fable, Pietr requested that the sessions be recorded. Recordings are useful in playing back scenes for learning purposes and providing evidence. It is important that permission is first sought before recording, like what Pietr did.

Another example stemmed from Govind's comments which triggered Olive's curiosity. Sometimes, when a colleague comments or makes a passing remark, you could pass off the comment as silly or not worth your time to follow up on. At other times, however, you may wish to enquire more, as was the case when Govind mentioned to Olive that she should propose her ideas to the Council. She became curious and followed up with Govind to find out more. Olive's single act of curiosity created an outcome that no one had thought possible.

In this fable, the use of a 360 tool was mentioned. There are many diagnostic or profiling tools that are available to help us deep dive into ourselves—to find out who we are, what drives us, what our strengths are, etc. The choice of a profiling tool is important. It may be useful to consider the following aspects when deciding on the tool for an organisation:

- What is the purpose of the tool?
- How will the tool help in creating a coaching culture?
- What are the costs involved?
- What support is required to implement the tool, internally and externally?
- What are the views of colleagues who have used the tool before?

To change the culture of an organisation, it may be necessary to invest in a tool that can work across the organisation, one that can be used at individual and team levels as well as across the organisation.

In summary, with the availability of evidence or data to help determine the root cause of the issue or crisis, the possibilities to arrive at how best to resolve the problem are wide-ranging. The decision-making process becomes smoother and faster. The next steps to achieve change become clearer. The use of profiling tools is now commonplace amongst many organisations. The decision to invest needs to be considered carefully—which tool to adopt, one that can be used across the organisation and by all employees to progress and develop.

LANGUAGE

"A different language is a different vision of life."
—Federico Fellini

Language is power. When used wisely, language can positively and deeply affect the mind, the heart, and the soul. The impact and power of language cannot be undermined when used to converse effectively with each other, in teams, and across the organisation. It is an essential tool for change.

In the WILD Framework, language refers to how we communicate our ideas and feelings with authenticity and with clarity, making every interaction count. It is about being authentic, building trust and respect, being mindful of our behaviour, and showing the care and empathy towards each other. A simple "how are you today" can mean a lot to a colleague. It is about learning new skills to achieve the goals that we desire.

Table 3 gives some questions to reflect on when implementing changes in language.

- Who can you lend a helping hand to at the workplace?
- Who can help you achieve your goals?
- What do you need to do differently in order to achieve a shared and collective leadership within your team?
- What needs to change to improve coaching conversations in your team or organisation?
- How would you engage with your stakeholders/customers?

Table 3. Some questions to ponder during the Language stage.

Building a new language requires getting rid of the old ways of speaking or communicating with each other that do not serve the best interests of the employees of an organisation. Those behaviours or interactions that create silos in organisations, create mistrust and disrespect can be changed through learning a new way of communicating with each other. Mutual support is crucial during this important phase. Most critical is the behaviour from the top—all the leaders must adopt the new language in their communication with employees. They must be role models of these new behaviours.

In the fable, a new language emerged for Lang, Govind, and the Triple C team as a result of the interventions they experienced. For Lang, hearing the story about The Three Questions impacted him deeply that he took immediate action to create a new language for himself. This new language

helped build effective engagement, with respect, encouragement, curiosity, and the willingness to learn from mistakes.

Having a support network with champions to help drive the new language across the organisation is essential in building a new culture. In the fable, the next generation of leaders namely Ting, Olive, and Aang became the WILD Company's champions to lead the charge towards embracing a new language, implementing training programmes to develop new skills amongst employees. The positive effect of using this new language at the town hall gave them the impetus to accelerate a culture of coaching and collaboration across the organisation.

The new language helped the WILD leaders to overcome their second crisis. Despite the overwhelming impact of the latest crisis that befell them, they were able to prevail over the situation by taking ownership of the challenge they had, working collaboratively, and showing one voice to the outside world. Their culture of being curious, courageous, and collaborative helped them to overcome the challenges they faced.

In summary, a new way of being is created with a new language. How this is embraced across the organisation depends on it starting at the very top. The head of the organisation, the CEO, the C-suite need to walk the talk and show up in a way that others will follow. The senior leaders are the role models that employees look up to. What better way to have an organisation change than through the collective efforts, consistent behaviours and actions of their senior leaders.

<u>D</u>EPLOYMENT

*"Deployment is nothing without decisiveness,
discipline, determination, and dedication."*
—Unknown

Culture at a workplace takes time to build and even longer to change. Deploying a culture change involves the whole organisation, from the top leadership through to every single employee. In creating or becoming a new culture where coaching conversations are the norm, coaching activities need to be built into the DNA of every employee so that individual conversations have an element of coaching in them. Just by being curious or asking questions to clarify and understand, showing one is listening to the conversation and not interrupting or preparing for a rebuttal, helps one take a step closer to achieving a coaching approach in conversations. But that is not enough.

In order to sustain the momentum of change, it is necessary to have the dedication of the leaders to be disciplined to continuously follow through and engage with all levels in the organisation. Even when changes in leadership happen—and they most often do—the importance of staying the course is crucial for the success of any culture change to be sustained.

Change takes time. In the fable, it took two years from the leaders being aware of the need to change, to being able to sustain the new culture. Skills training needs to be a priority, continuously and regularly implemented for every employee to be armed with the necessary tools to behave in a way that is consistent with the company values. Table 4 gives some guiding questions towards sustaining a new culture in an organisation.

- How can you best prioritise the activities that you plan to work on?
- What indicators will help confirm that you are working in a high-value creating team?
- What does it take to sustain a coaching culture in your organisation?
- What measures have you put in place to assess success?
- How will you know that you are on target to achieving your goals?

Table 4. Some questions to ponder during the Deployment stage.

Because the culture of coaching was already embedded deep into the organisation, when the next crisis hit, the leaders took ownership to resolve the issue. A team was immediately formed and worked effectively together to investigate and come up with solutions to resolve the crisis. There was no finger-pointing, no blaming; just an acceptance that an unfortunate incident occurred, that needed fixing. Everyone realised that the impact could be serious, not only affecting the WILD Company but their customers and their employees.

On the other hand, the NEON Company failed to survive the crisis. The behaviours of the leaders were reminiscent of what happened at the WILD Company two years before. Had they the wisdom to realise how detrimental bad behaviours are, perhaps with the best technical expertise available, they may have been able to ride out the crisis. That did not happen for them unfortunately.

Changing the culture in any organisation takes time. But in today's fast-paced environment, time is of the essence. Leaders may not have the luxury of time to make a lasting impact. They may also change roles, within the organisation or to an external organisation. It is important to note that any change in culture needs more than just the leaders. A clear plan of action has to be put in place from the very start of the implementation of the culture change. Another important factor is the engagement of the organisation in implementing the change. It is more than just the leaders who are important in enabling change. It is of equal importance to have followers too.

In addition, for any change to be sustainable, opportunities must be created for communities to have conversations, to communicate, share ideas and views. These activities need to happen repeatedly, in multiple instances over time across the whole organisation. One such opportunity is having a community space, physical or virtual, where staff are invited to get together. In the fable, organising the Koko Kara Café after the town hall was an opportunity for staff to contemplate, reflect, and dialogue with their colleagues on the topics that were shared by the leaders, issues that matter to them individually and collectively. On that day, the senior leaders participated in the same event, giving all staff the opportunity to engage with them, to share their views and ideas, and have a chance to get to know them better. This idea is already happening through the concept of the World Café methodology—a simple, effective, and flexible format that enables large group dialogues to take place.

In the fable, volunteers came forward to support the culture change—champions of change, or leader-coaches, were identified and trained to help bring forward the movement towards a new culture of coaching. In essence, the whole organisation is galvanised to make the change happen. That is when a new culture will be created—a culture that embraces coaching as a means of operating by all employees in the company.

In summary, with deliberate, definitive, and dedicated discipline, the deployment of actions that leads to the successful creation of a coaching culture will be achieved. This is a culture where leaders consistently walk the talk, where they are role models to the rest of the organisation, and where they embrace the concept of making every interaction count.

There are no difficult people.
There are just people wanting to be understood,
appreciated, respected, and valued.

RESOURCES AND BIBLIOGRAPHY

BOOKS

The Arbinger Institute. *Leadership and Self Deception: Getting Out of the Box.* Berrett-Koehler Publishers, 2002.

Blanchard, Ken, and Spencer Johnson. *The New One Minute Manager.* William Morrow, 2015.

Clutterbuck, David. *Coaching the Team at Work.* Nicholas Brealy International, 2007.

Clutterbuck, David, et al. *Building and Sustaining a Coaching Culture.* Chartered Institute of Personnel and Development, 2016.

Forman, Dawn, et al, editors. *Creating a Coaching Culture for Managers in Your Organisation.* Routledge, 2013.

George, Bill, and Peter Sims. *True North: Discover Your Authentic Leadership.* Jossey-Bass, 2007.

Hawkins, Peter. *Creating a Coaching Culture: Developing a Coaching Strategy for Your Organisation.* McGraw-Hill Education, 2012.

Hawkins, Peter. *Leadership Team Coaching: Developing Collective Transformational Leadership.* 3rd ed., Kogan Page, 2017.

Hawkins, Peter. *Leadership Team Coaching in Practice: Case Studies on Developing High-performing Team.* 2nd ed., Kogan Page, 2018.

Johnson, Spencer. *Who Moved My Cheese?* GP Putnam's Sons, 2002.

Jones, Gillian, and Ro Gorell. *How to Create A Coaching Culture: A Practical Introduction.* 2nd ed., Kogan Page in association with Chartered Institute of Personnel and Development, 2018.

Kofman, Fred. *Conscious Business: How to Build Value Through Values.* Sounds True, 2006.

Kotter, John, and Holger Rathgeber. *That's Not How We Do It Here!: A Story About How Organizations Rise and Fall—And Can Rise Again.* Portfolio/Penguin, 2016.

Landsberg, Max. *The Tao of Coaching: Boost Your Effectiveness at Work by Inspiring and Developing Those Around You.* Profile Books, 2015.

Lencioni, Patrick. *The Advantage: Why Organizational Health Trumps Everything Else In Business.* Jossey-Bass, 2012.

Lencioni, Patrick. *The Five Dysfunctions of a Team: A Leadership Fable.* Jossey-Bass, 2002.

Rimanoczy, Isabel, and Ernie Turner. *Action Reflection Learning*[TM]*: Solving Real Business Problems by Connecting Learning with Earning.* Davies-Black Publishing, 2008.

Skiffington, Suzanne, and Perry Zeus. *Behavioural Coaching: How to Build Sustainable Personal and Organizational Strength.* McGraw-Hill, 2003.

Tolstoy, Leo. *The Gospel in Tolstoy: Selections from His Short Stories, Spiritual Writings, and Novels,* edited by Miriam LeBlanc. Plough Publishing House, 2015.

Tucker, Kenneth A., and Vandana Allman. *Animals Inc.: A Business Fable for the 21st Century.* Warner Business Books, 2004.

Turner, Ernie. *Gentle Interventions for Team Coaching: Little Things that Make a BIG Difference.* LIM LLC, 2013.

PAPERS AND JOURNAL ARTICLES

Anderson, Merrill C., et al. *Creating Coaching Cultures: What Business Leaders Expect and Strategies to Get There.* Center for Creative Leadership White Paper, 2009, http://cclinnovation.org/wp-content/uploads/2020/03/creatingcoachingcultures.pdf. Accessed April 2021.

Bianco-Mathis, Virginia, and Nabors L. "Building a Coaching Organization". *Human Capital/TD at Work*, vol. 33, issue 1605, May 2016.

Filipkowski, Jenna, et al. *Building a Coaching Culture for Increased Employee Engagement.* International Coach Federation (ICF) and Human Capital Institute (HCI), 2015. https://www.hci.org/research/building-coaching-culture-increased-employee-engagement. Accessed April 2021.

Filipkowski, Jenna, et al. *Building a Coaching Culture with Managers and Leaders.* International Coach Federation (ICF) and Human Capital Institute (HCI), 2016, https://www.hci.org/research/building-coaching-culture-managers-and-leaders. Accessed April 2021.

Filipkowski, Jenna, et al. *Building a Coaching Culture with Millennial Leaders.* International Coach Federation (ICF) and Human Capital Institute (HCI), 2017, https://www.hci.org/research/building-coaching-culture-millennial-leaders. Accessed April 2021.

Filipkowski, Jenna, et al. *Building a Coaching Culture for Change Management.* International Coach Federation (ICF) and Human Capital Institute (HCI), 2018, https://www.hci.org/research/building-coaching-culture-change-management. Accessed April 2021.

Filipkowski, Jenna, et al. *Building Strong Coaching Cultures for the Future.* International Coaching Federation (ICF) and Human Capital Institute (HCI), 2019, https://www.hci.org/research/building-strong-coaching-cultures-future. Accessed April 2021.

Hart, E. Wayne. *Developing a Coaching Culture. Centre for Creative Leadership*, 2003, http://citeseerx.ist.psu.edu/viewdoc/download?-doi=10.1.1.197.234&rep=rep1&type=pdf. Accessed April 2021.

International Coach Federation (ICF) and Human Capital Institute (HCI). *Building a Coaching Culture.* 2014, https://researchportal.coachfederation.org/Document/Pdf/1313.pdf. Accessed April 2021.

Riddle, Douglas. *Truth and Courage: Implementing a Coaching Culture with Better Conversations Every Day. Center for Creative Leadership White Paper*, 2018, https://www.ccl.org/wp-content/uploads/2016/08/Truth-and-Courage-CCL-White-Paper.pdf. Accessed April 2021.

WEBSITES

The World Café. The World Café Community Foundation, 2021, http://www.theworldcafe.com/. Accessed April 2021.

ACKNOWLEDGEMENTS

We are extremely grateful to our awesome family members, colleagues, and friends who have been with us throughout the book writing process.

FROM CHOY KIEW

My life partner, Yee Sun, and Colin, our son—I am filled with so much good fortune to have your love, wisdom, thoughtfulness, kindness, and patience. I look back with humility, pride, and much joy on the years we spent in Japan and China, how our experiences have shaped who we are today and what beautiful memories we bring forward to mould ourselves into a future filled with peace, happiness, and fulfilment.

My dearest friend and confidante, Sarojini Devi. From the very bottom of my heart, thank you for being with me every step of my journey as an author and an entrepreneur. Your wise words, candid views, and very open feedback are much treasured and valued. BFFs forever!!!

Deepa Desai—what can I say but that we were meant to meet in this lifetime. Our bond is amazing and through the short number of years we have known each other, our friendship has grown. You are such a beautiful human being, Deepa. Thank you for being you and coming into my life.

To my colleagues in AstraZeneca, who have been with me during my twenty-seven years of learning and discovery in a fantastic organisation. It is indeed my honour and privilege to have been your colleague on this amazing journey of personal growth and development.

- To David Brennan, you have shown me what it truly means for a CEO to walk the talk and how to make every interaction count. I am still in awe and will be forever grateful for that five-minute conversation which helped transform my view of what great leadership is all about.
- To my line managers who have challenged me to live my potential to the fullest, specifically Ross Horsburgh, John Stevens, Bertil Lindmark, Sven Ohlman, Steve Yang, Lena Vagberg. You have been instrumental in helping me discover my strengths and capabilities. To Ross in particular, without your strong challenges, I would not be who I am today. It took me a long time to realise this but I am so glad I did!
- To my Samurai Seven: Sachiko Kameo, Shuji Hada, Michitaka Sasai, Shigeyuki Yamaji, Norihisa Sakiyama, Yukiko Ochi, Iwami Nakatani. From the very bottom of my heart, thank you for your warm welcome to AZKK and the support each of you gave me. You are such a wonderful team to work with, and I have been so fortunate to learn so much from you all.
- Angie Loo, Anna Ordinario, Kazuko Kasahara, Rajender Kumar, Ranju Sharma, Yoko Iwai, Kazuhiro Sasahara, Takaharu Hino—your passion in building a leader-coach culture within your teams and functions will forever be engraved in my memory. Thank you for the fun times we had as well as the serious and fantastic dialogue sessions!
- Birte Sebastian, thank you for inspiring in me the importance of effective communication at a corporate as well as personal level. I am grateful to you for being in my life at a truly remarkable time, with

adventures in Japan and China that were fun, unforgettable, and with so many memorable moments.

- My coaches and mentors, Ernie Turner, Mary Moore, Peter Karlsson—I am truly, truly blessed to have been coached and mentored by you. Your words, questions, and insights have touched me in so many ways. I am so very privileged to have had the opportunity to stand on the shoulders of giants.

FROM AILEEN:

To Steven, my other half, for everything you have done, especially in recent years, and teaching me to live life for myself (self-care), to do what I really wanted, and to achieve my writing dream. To my children—Samantha, Melissa, and Louis—for giving me love, happiness, fun, laughter, pain and sadness, and more. You created a colourful rainbow of life experiences that enriched me as your mother in so many ways, with wonderful memories to treasure.

To Bente Dyring, my line manager at Danfoss Asia Pacific, who first introduced me to how we, as HR leaders, can use coaching effectively to support our business leaders at the workplace.

To Anne Welsh, my coach extraordinaire and mentor. Thank you for giving me the opportunity to personally experience the magic and value of coaching. Also for your dedication and care to coach and mentor me during a very difficult phase of my life, helping me gain the clarity and courage I needed to face and deal with my challenges as you supported me.

To my many colleagues at GlaxoSmithKline (GSK) in our Asia regional office in Singapore and our corporate HQ in London, who taught me what a coaching culture within an organisation looked like, sounded like, and felt like—what a coaching culture across an organisation can do for its employees at all levels of the organisation. This has inspired me to embark on coaching as a career after my days at GSK, and to pursue the ambition to create coaching cultures within workplaces.

To Lin Tan from Collective Change Institute who invited me to join the ICW 2020 organising team with the ICF Singapore Chapter. This voluntary project brought me, Adrian, and Choy Kiew together which resulted in us working together, setting up The Coaching Culture organisation and co-authoring this book.

FROM ADRIAN:

To my dearest wife, Agnes, and daughter, Andrea—thank you for being my cheer squad and helping with editing. When I first spoke about writing a book, both of you were extremely supportive and enthusiastic. Thank you for all the love, hope, joy, and faith that you have given me. I could not have done this without the both of you.

To my parents Felix and Pauline, brother Mark, sister-in-law Janice, and godchildren—your unwavering love, patience, and prayers have kept me going. Thank you for journeying with me through my career highs and lows, your encouragement, and faith in me.

The Brief Academy community of Solution Focused coaches in Singapore and Malaysia, led by Simon Lee. Thank you for supporting me through my coach training journey, in particular Alvin Ng for inspiring and encouraging me to follow in your footsteps.

My career mentors Phil Ventimiglia formerly from Dell, Piet Coelewij and Fabio Offredi formerly from Philips—thank you for instilling in me the qualities of relentless creativity, extensive collaboration, passionate customer focus, and authentic connections.

FROM THE AUTHORS:

Thank you Stefan Nicholas Ng, for sharing your knowledge in explaining the characteristics and behaviours of the animals at Wildlife Reserves

Singapore. We sincerely hope that we have done justice to the information you imparted to us so readily and with so much passion and love for the animals under your care.

Thank you Paul Goh, our photographer, for taking all those beautiful photographs of us in the "wild". Your professionalism put us at ease and your creativity is simply "roar-some"!

Jeraldine Boh, industrial design student extraordinaire—you are a star! Your creativity is amazing. Your designs powerful and impactful. It has been a real delight working with you. Thank you for appearing so magically at the right time just when we were looking for an illustrator.

Michael Boey and Eve Thow, your invaluable comments on our early draft were spot-on and very astute. We truly appreciate your time and patience in reading and reviewing our story in its unpolished state filled with spelling and grammatical errors.

Our thanks to Phoon Kok Hwa and Patricia Ng from Candid Creation Publishing for their sound advice, professional editorial support, and keen insights in helping us perfect the structure, content, and language of our book. We truly appreciate the challenge you may have faced working with three authors at the same time who share a consummate passion to write about our experiences in creating a coaching culture with the world.

Thank you to the ICF Singapore Chapter Executive Council 2020 & 2021 and the community of coaches for checking in and cheering us on.

Fellow authors Elliott Lee, Chung Yin Wah, Michelle Ow, from Team Everest—we had fun learning and climbing "Mount Everest" together.

A big thank you to our clients and coachees for cheering us on, supporting us, and allowing us to test our Framework. We could not have completed this book without you.

THE GENESIS

What could possibly happen when three coaches come together? What could we talk about? Coaching, of course! Thankfully, there was more than coaching that dominated our conversations. We three coaches had a strong desire to share the impact and benefits of coaching with everyone and have it found everywhere, from workplaces to homes and communities in society.

That led to the birth of The Coaching Culture.

ABOUT THE COACHING CULTURE

The Coaching Culture is a Singapore-based boutique coaching and consultancy practice of Asian origin. We partner with each client to co-create a bespoke leadership development programme for teams and individuals based on our proprietary WILD Framework. We specialise in team coaching, executive coaching, corporate training, and facilitation. Founded by Adrian Lim, Aileen Chee, and Cheong Choy Kiew, three International Coaching Federation (ICF) credentialled coaches, we co-create and deliver bespoke solutions for clients.

With over eighty years of collective commercial experience in marketing, learning and talent development, clinical development and quality assurance, we offer a plethora of 360 assessment, personality, psychometric and facilitation tools, and coaching methodologies. These include Systemic Team Coaching and TC360 (developed by Professor Peter Hawkins), Shared Leadership Team Coaching (developed by Ernie Turner), Solution Focused Coaching, Genos Emotional Intelligence, Emergenetics, Soundwave and LEGO® Serious Play.

We share a common purpose and aspiration—to make Singapore and the world a better place in which to live, work, and play. We want to share our knowledge and experience in coaching while imparting the importance of creating a coaching culture in a simple and relatable way.

OUR LOGO

The logo is a stylised calligraphy of the Chinese character 心 (xīn) which means heart; mind; soul. Every interaction, be it with our clients or partners, comes from the heart.

The brushstrokes are modern and progressive. Their varying thickness symbolises the delicate balance between boldness, agility, flexibility, and generosity. The golden orange brushstrokes represents us, the three founders, and our rich Asian heritage. The deep blue brushstroke is the letter "C" in coaching and culture, the essence of our purpose. It also represents the coming together of our diverse professional experiences and global perspectives to co-create sustainable solutions for our clients.

OUR VISION

The Coaching Culture aims to create a movement. A movement that finds its way into workplaces, homes, and society where every individual has the opportunity to create and experience coaching moments, to coach someone or to be coached. Anytime. Everywhere.

Our approach touches three areas namely, Communities, Education, and Organisations, or CEO for short.

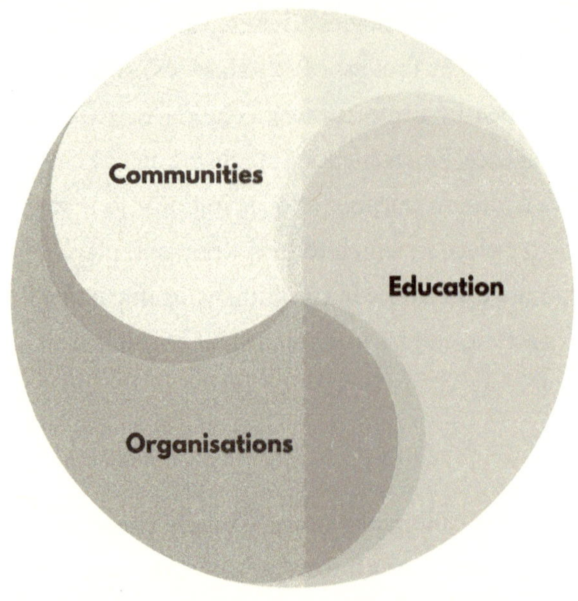

- **Communities**

  We give back to the various communities in society by delivering workshops, organising talks and webinars, and offering low-bono coaching opportunities.

  The WILD Framework remains at the core of all these initiatives. It provides a road map for communities to create a coaching culture by arousing an awareness of the need to change, identifying the gaps, learning a new language, and deploying change.

  Now is the time for everyone to seize the opportunity to emerge stronger from the Covid-19 pandemic and take ownership of our lives.

- **Education**

  Our book, *Into the WILD*, and future ones to come will serve as educational tools. *Into the WILD* begins with a fable based on the WILD

Framework. It is a beginner's guide to creating a coaching culture at home, at workplaces, and in the various communities in society, one step at a time.

- **Organisation**

We support professionals in organisations, big and small, from multinational corporations to small and medium enterprises including family-owned businesses. We provide one-on-one, team, and organisational coaching. As we support these professionals and teams, we are hopeful that the benefits of coaching will naturally extend to their families and friends. Coaching changes lives.

To find out more about us and what we do, please scan the QR code on the left or go to our website at **https://www.thecoachingculture.co.** You can also drop us an email at **contact@thecoachingculture.co.** We look forward to partnering and supporting you on your journey to creating a coaching culture.

ABOUT THE AUTHORS

CHEONG CHOY KIEW

Choy Kiew has over thirty years of working experience in senior leadership positions across the Asia-Pacific, Europe, and South Africa. She has established a record of developing, mentoring, coaching, and motivating colleagues and teams to excel in their performance and in delivering outstanding value to the business.

Choy Kiew started her career as a statistician in the Singapore Ministry of Health. It was in AstraZeneca, where she spent twenty-seven years of her career, that she developed her capabilities in leading across complex, multi-country, multi-ethnic organisational structures within the Asia-Pacific region. During her career in AstraZeneca, she has lived and worked in Japan and in China. Her last corporate role was in IQVIA, heading the Quality Assurance team in the Asia-Pacific, Europe, and South Africa.

In 2019, Choy Kiew left the corporate world to kick-start a new career as an executive coach. She is an ICF credentialled Associate Certified Coach (ACC) and has also obtained certification as a Shared Leadership Team Coach with Leadership In Motion.

Choy Kiew coaches executives to develop their leadership potential and to live a life of authenticity, both at the workplace and the home front. She works with teams to achieve high performance through effective collaboration and communication, where the culture and values of the organisation are built into the core of every employee. Her coaching philosophy is based on continuous learning and growth whilst optimising every relationship, making every interaction count. Coaching with Choy Kiew is result-focused.

AILEEN CHEE

Aileen has over thirty years of experience in Leadership Development, Organisational Development, Talent Management, Performance Management, and Commercial Key Account Management with multinational corporations and local conglomerates spanning industries from engineering and manufacturing, to supply chain, IT, professional services, and pharmaceuticals. She specialises in partnering with business leaders to identify, develop, and retain high potentials to grow succession talent pipelines for key business roles, to drive and sustain business strategies.

Aileen is an ICF credentialled Associate Certified Coach (ACC). She is also a SoundWave® certified Practitioner Coach, a StrengthsAsia certified Strengths® Facilitator and a Breakthrough Coaching Enhanced Practitioner.

As a Career Coach, Aileen works with professionals to help them gain clarity about their career ambition and to create a development road map for success. She also works with organisations to improve business performance by maximising high performance and creating rewarding team and work environments.

Aileen's approach to leadership development and coaching is focused on engaging key stakeholders to understand why they need the change, identify what needs to be changed, and follow through the change process to measure growth in leadership effectiveness. Her coaching philosophy is outcome-focused and strengths-based.

Fluent in both Mandarin and English, Aileen has led and managed remote teams across Asia-Pacific countries. She has accumulated an in-depth appreciation of global mindfulness, developed cultural diversity and sensitivity to international business practices across the Asia-Pacific, the Middle East, the UK, USA, and Canada.

ADRIAN LIM

Adrian has over twenty years of global and regional marketing management experience across the consumer electronics, telecommunications, and IT solutions industries. He specialises in strategic marketing, go-to-market strategy, product management, e-commerce, branding, and communications.

Some of his leadership roles include Regional Director of Industry Solutions and Marketing at LG Electronics, and Global Director of Go-to-market and Product Management at Dell. Adrian has also served as Head of Marketing at Wincor Nixdorf and REC Solar and had career stints at Motorola, Philips, Sony, and AIA.

Adrian is an ICF credentialled Professional Certified Coach (PCC), Mentor Coach, and Coaching Supervisor. He is also an EMCC certified (Systemic) Team Coach, a certified Solution Focused Coach, a Marshall Goldsmith Stakeholder Centered Leadership Executive Coach, a Genos Emotional Intelligence Practitioner, an Emergenetics Associate, and a LEGO® Serious Play facilitator.

Adrian coaches executives to develop their leadership potential and define a road map for success, as well as works with teams to maximise high performance and create rewarding team environments. He also works with individuals in a group context to develop collaborative peer relationships, share knowledge, and build capabilities across the organisation. His systemic approach to executive development and coaching includes a strong emphasis on involvement of stakeholders, implementation of change and follow-through to measure growth in leadership effectiveness.

Fluent in both Mandarin and English, Adrian has coached physical and virtual teams and professionals globally. He has also accumulated an in-depth appreciation of international mindfulness, cultural diversity, and business practices in Asia and around the world.